AFRO-BRAZILIAN
NUMEROLOGY

AFRO-BRAZILIAN
NUMEROLOGY

Awakening Your Better Self with the Wisdom of the Orishas

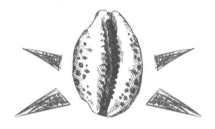

DIEGO DE OXÓSSI

Destiny Books
Rochester, Vermont

Destiny Books
One Park Street
Rochester, Vermont 05767
www.DestinyBooks.com

Text stock is SFI certified

Destiny Books is a division of Inner Traditions International

Copyright 2022 © by Diego de Oxóssi

Originally published in Portuguese in 2021 under the title *Odus de Nascimento: Desvende Sua Personalidade Com o Mapa Astral dos Orixás* by Editora Arole Cultural
First U.S. edition published in 2022 by Destiny Books

Cataloging-in-Publication Data for this title is available from the Library of Congress

ISBN 978-1-64411-594-7 (print)
ISBN 978-1-64411-595-4 (ebook)

Printed and bound in the United States by Lake Book Manufacturing, Inc.
The text stock is SFI certified. The Sustainable Forestry Initiative® program promotes sustainable forest management.

10 9 8 7 6 5 4 3 2 1

Text design and layout by Virginia Scott Bowman
This book was typeset in Garamond Premier Pro with Fnord used as the display typeface

To send correspondence to the author of this book, mail a first-class letter to the author c/o Inner Traditions • Bear & Company, One Park Street, Rochester, VT 05767, and we will forward the communication, or contact the author directly at **www.diegodeoxossi.com.br.**

Your vision will become clear only when you look into your heart. Who looks outside, dreams; who looks inside, wakes up.

CARL JUNG (1895–1961)

Contents

PART 3
Awakening Your Better Self

Special Thanks

Afro-Brazilian Numerology is dedicated to my mother, Marines, and my sister, Camila, who even from a distance have always found ways to allow me to dream and realize, and especially to my grandmother Nelza Brito Flores, who first introduced me to spirituality and who made her return to Orun in the month of its first edition release in Portuguese.

To Priestess Ieda de Ogun, for all the affection and companionship in these more than ten years together and for the simplicity of her words, full of great life and priesthood lessons. To the warrior Anderson de Ogun, who supports me in every battle of life and believes in the mission that the Orishas assigned us. And to dear Aluísio, who says he learns daily with me but cannot imagine how much he teaches me.

To Eshu 7 Facadas—my friend, my drunken Rascal, and my eternal guardian—and Oshossi, the hunter of a single arrow, master of the jungle and of my life, for everything: for the Kingdom, for the world, for existing! And to everyone who encouraged or doubted me, both are my daily fuel!

1

If You Don't Know Where You're Going, Any Road Can Take You There

First of all, welcome and congratulations! If you are reading these words, it is because you have made one of the most important decisions of your life: to look inside yourself, understand what makes you exactly the way you are, and, especially, to dive deeply into the mysteries of your soul to unveil what prevents you from achieving happiness! Talking like that may seem magical or easy, but believe me: it takes a lot of courage to truly take this step, and I believe you have that courage, even though it may feel like it's asleep.

From now on, I will guide you on a journey of self-knowledge, and in the end, you will certainly not be the same person who is reading these words now. However, you need to make two lifetime commitments to yourself.

THE FIRST AGREEMENT

Our first agreement is that you will never again believe the biggest lie that exists and that, I am sure, you have been saying repeatedly throughout your life: *Things happen to me because the world or someone did (or said or felt or thought) something.*

Other versions are: *I am not lucky in life because the world or someone did (or said or felt or thought) something. Things in my life go wrong because the world or someone did (or said or felt or thought) something.*

Never again allow yourself to believe any lying phrase that shifts responsibility for what happens in your life to anyone other than you.

You are solely responsible for the life you've been living!

I'm not saying there are no external factors that influence our lives, whether they are of a practical nature, such as moving to another city or losing or getting a job, or subtle and subjective issues, such as jealousy or envy of others or even the effect of negative spells against us. But even if in many situations we have no control over what happens to us, in absolutely every situation we have numerous alternatives about *what we do and how we feel about what happened.*

Let me tell you a real story: About five years ago, a woman came to see me for a consultation with cowrie shell divination. She had assumed a leadership position at work and complained that every day her colleagues and subordinates would not accept her position and persecuted and humiliated her. During the divination, the Odus Oshe and Owarin—both in their negative aspect—confirmed her complaint, indicating exactly the situation she described. Furthermore, she had Odu Ossa as a regent Odu in the two main positions of her Orisha birth chart: Odu Ori and Osogbo Ori (don't worry, you'll learn what this means later). This indicated a perfect scenario for having conflicts and power struggles with other women in all areas of her life.

Once the problem was identified, which in this case had an external origin, we waited a few days and later did the necessary rituals to neutralize the negative influence of the Odus, which the divination had shown. The conflicts at work calmed down, her authority was once again recognized by her colleagues, and her life got back on track.

From then on, every three or four months the same woman came to see me for a new consultation. Each time she came with complaints similar to the original one but with new characters and plots. On her next consultation, she reported that she was dating the director of the company and now, in addition to professional issues, she added persecutions and disputes caused by coworkers' and subordinates' jealousy of her relationship with the director. In these new divinations, no Odu appeared to provide spiritual care; instead, all the advice offered was for emotional matters, guiding her on how to respond to the adverse events happening to her.

Almost a year and a half after the first consultation, Eshu—through Odu Obara, the path of prosperity and happiness—indicated that she should leave her job for new opportunities that had risen, among them to be a project consultant in her area of expertise. This time, we conducted a huge ritual to Odu Obara to enhance the professional growth indicated by the cowrie shell divination.

For the next two years I didn't hear from her. Then she appeared, wanting to consult the cowries again with familiar complaints about the same people from the same job. The relationship with the director had ended, and the persecutions and humiliations were happening again. The situation had actually worsened. We started the consultation, but no cowrie shell opened. Eshu had nothing to say about the situation!

"How can that be?" she asked indignantly, caught between anger and tears. "I am having a serious problem! I can't take another day being so humiliated, and the Orishas don't say anything?" I asked Eshu for permission to pose a new question, despite His initial negative response, and Eshu bluntly answered: *What I have to say has already been said. What had to be done (spiritually) has already been done. What has she done with everything I have given her?*

Even considering the bad character of some of her coworkers . . . Even considering the woman's Birth Odus, which really brought constant persecution in all areas of her life since childhood . . . And even considering that, in this period of almost five years between the first and the last consultation, numerous positive and negative situations happened to her. . . . Who, after all, chose to continue living a toxic and destructive reality?

Can you see how, despite outer influences, ultimately, we are solely responsible for everything that happens to us? It's like my father used to say: Not to make any decision is, also, to make one!

The truth is that the events of our day-to-day lives are not fatalities or coincidences of fate: they are more or less positive results of the decisions we make—or fail to make—and this whole process has a name: self-responsibility!

Maybe I shouldn't say it like that, so openly at the beginning of the book, but it's for your sake: I've been exactly where you are today, with the same anxieties and the same bunch of questions that you have at this very moment. I also doubted it when I first heard that I am responsible for everything that happens to me. And I also hoped that working with the birth Odus and the Orisha birth chart would magically solve my problems without me having to consciously examine who I was until I could become who I am.

All the stories and experiences you will read in this book are real, and everything you will learn here was experienced in practice. Our first agreement is the most important lesson so that what we'll see next makes sense in your life—as it did in mine. Of course, the first time that I swallowed my complaints about the outer world due to my frustrations and I stopped for a few minutes to understand what my responsibility for all of that was, it was painful—but also liberating! When I started to understand that if pain was inevitable, suffering was optional, I became able to avoid mistakes and frustrations before they even happened. And that feels like magic.

I don't know about you, but I've always loved fantasy movies like the Harry Potter series or those with magical and esoteric themes. In fact, I must confess, even though I come from a spiritualist family, the great trigger for me to start studying and practicing magic was the film *The Craft*. It was exciting to see those girls in the middle of the forest performing rituals, materializing their desires through spells and achieving their desired goals, no matter how silly those goals seemed to be. But, as inspiring as that could be, it was necessary to admit that it was just a movie and in real life our desires don't materialize like a miracle to the eyes.

THE SECOND AGREEMENT

If you're reading this book, it's because, just like me, you believe in the power of the Orishas, and you know that magic exists and that the power of spells is true. What few people will tell you is that the results of these spells are linked to the effort you are willing to undertake to make your wish come true. Therefore, our second agreement is as follows: if you want to truly transform your life and awaken the best version of yourself, then you need to admit that this will only be possible through personal effort and that to get where you really want to be you must pay the price of life.

Because most people do not commit to these two agreements they continue to experience the same problems over and over again, even if they change jobs or end a relationship. In their version of the world, they never make mistakes. The blame for their insults is always on others, and any effort seems too much because they expect a miracle to come from heaven and change everything around them, as long as they don't need to change anything about themselves. But when it comes time to roll up their sleeves and take their own life in their hands, treading the path that they've asked the Orishas for so many times, they give up before the first drop of sweat runs off their faces!

Once again: You are the only one responsible for the life you have lived until today, and everything you have achieved so far is the result of your choices—or the lack of them! If your current reality is not what you wanted and if you are the only one responsible for it, then you are also the only one who can change this situation.

A PERSONAL TRANSFORMATION TOOL

Know yourself and you will know the universe.

This saying and its variations have been known since ancient Egypt and are written at the entrance to Luxor Temple—one of the oldest and best-known temples of magic and wisdom on Earth. It represents one of life's great truths, serving as a guide for searching our deepest goals: our reality reflects the ways we are, think, and act. For this reason, knowing yourself is the first step to achieving happiness.

From now on, this old lesson will make even more sense in your life, and the biggest mistake you've been making so far is to ignore it: like a big invisible network of energies, absolutely everything in the universe as we know it is connected and related to one another, which includes the events in your life, the way you relate to people, and the situations in which you find yourself. So, what if you could predict some of these situations before they happen? Even better, what if you could change the way you react to what happens to you and, in that way, change the whole course of events in the future?

The truth is that your future will be a pure and simple result of what you do today. Understanding the energies that rule your birth and the influence they have on your personality and the ways you interact with day-to-day life can change how you perceive yourself and how you relate to the world around you.

Most successful people I know say that, at some point in their lives, they went through a deep process of inner searching, seeking to know themselves better through tools, such as oracles, birth charts, or spiritual guides. Like those seekers, you're one step closer to starting this journey and becoming able to transform your reality and the way you live.

On the journey to unveil your soul and awaken the best version of yourself, you may have already consulted cowrie shells or the tarot when doubts crossed your mind. Or perhaps you have even done the necessary rituals to balance negative energies that you may have identified. But none of that matters if you continue to focus all your efforts on understanding the *outer* energies that influence your destiny without examining how they combine with the *inner energies* that have guided you since birth. If you look only to the outside, I'm sorry to say, you will be doomed to repeatedly experience the same problems over and over again.

When I first saw it happening, I almost didn't believe it. As I came to understand that the situations in my life followed behavior patterns, and made conscious efforts to break those patterns, I was able to completely change the outcome of these situations and the way I dealt with the day-to-day difficulties. Consequently, actions flowed better in my life, and I was able to accomplish more. The deeper I got into it, the more I was able to anticipate the challenges around me, the ways I dealt with them, and their results.

I'm sure you have heard that we live in a world of energies. Even science, through quantum physics, has found evidence that the vibrations of objects, people, and situations around us directly influence our lives. However, what most people who say this do not understand is that our personal vibrations and energies also influence and modify the outer world. These inner energies, which define and differentiate us from any other human in the world, are what we call birth Odus.

To conquer the largest mountain in the world, a climber needs a lot of willpower and stamina as well as the necessary equipment. Likewise, to meet this challenge of discovering your inner self, you need both determination and the right tools—and this is where the Orisha birth chart comes in. The chart is a powerful tool that will help you to discover your intrinsic qualities and learn the best ways to explore your potential on a daily basis. In the next chapters you will learn to analyze your birth Odus and the influence they have on different areas of life, allowing you to know and understand the positive and negative aspects of these energies and your ways of loving and relating, expressing yourself with people, dealing with professional and financial issues, and facing the challenges of destiny.

The birth Odus act like the signs in a horoscope, in this case an African horoscope. At the same time, in addition to the energy of each

Odu, each is connected to or provides a conduit for specific Orishas, and these Odus and Orishas influence us in all aspects of our existence. Therefore, two people with the same regent Odu in one of the Orisha birth chart major houses, such as Oju Ori (personality) or Osogbo Ori (the challenges for the inner revolution), will be influenced differently by the joint action of the observed house's Odu, of other Odus in their charts, and of the Orishas that manifest in them.

But there is no point in having an excellent tool in your hands if you don't know how to use it correctly. First, we will learn some important concepts about what the birth chart is and how to use it and its many features. A central concept is that Odus are roads for the flow of energies to circulate between Orun (the African heaven) and Aiye (Earth), and like any road, it takes its travelers from one place to another.

Whenever I think of the transformations I want in my life and of the Odus as roads leading to these transformations, I remember an excerpt from *Alice in Wonderland* by Lewis Carroll, when Alice meets the Cheshire Cat.

> "Would you tell me please which way I ought to go from here?"
>
> "That depends a good deal on where you want to get to," said the Cat.
>
> "I don't much care where—" said Alice.
>
> "Then it doesn't matter which way you go," said the Cat.
>
> "—so long as I get *somewhere*," Alice added as an explanation.
>
> "Oh, you're sure to do that," said the Cat, "if you only walk long enough."

For those who don't know where they're going, any path will do. If you are determined to understand the dynamics that the spiritual world has in your choices and decisions and to walk a new path in your life, two questions are fundamental for you to be able to get the best out of the tool you now have in hand.

Where are you now?
And where, after all, do you really want to go?

Before continuing to read this book, stop for a moment and meditate on your answers to these simple but important questions. Continue reading only after you have truly answered them. You will then be ready to discover your inner world and start building a path of success and happiness in your life. Know yourself, and you will know the universe . . . Remember?

For your inner transformation to really begin, in addition to the agreements you have just made, there is one last important and fundamental agreement to be made: the sincere commitment to recognize yourself as unique and special in such a huge universe and, with that, accept that you and everyone else are all in a process of constant improvement and evolution.

Even though the objective of this book is to teach you how to create and interpret the Orisha birth chart for yourself and anyone else, every change can only start from within. Therefore, the time has come to make a commitment between your conscious self and your soul, which is about to wake up. On the next page you will find a Letter of Personal Commitment. Read it carefully and more than once. After reading it, as a contract between you and yourself, write your full name on the first line of the letter. That done, take a deep breath and read it again, this time out loud, and sign on the last line, formalizing this intimate contract, which will surely yield good results going forward.

() *Letter of Personal Commitment*

I, _____, sign this Letter of Personal Commitment to myself, in a personal and sincere way, recognizing that from now on I will be the only person responsible for what happens in my life.

I understand and accept that many of the situations experienced in daily life are beyond my power, but that over all of them, I always have the choice to hang on or let it go.

I recognize that until today I have often resisted admitting that much suffering and pain could have been avoided or changed if I had had the courage to look sincerely inward and face my shadow.

Still, I don't blame myself for that. I am human, and because of that, I am constantly learning and evolving. Therefore, I make this commitment with me from now on in the name of my own happiness.

From this moment on, I free myself of all the negative burdens of the past and consciously decide to know myself and awaken the best version of me.

Signed me, on the first day of the best year of my life!

_____

2

How to Use This Book

To better understand African spirituality, the way Odu and Orisha magic is practiced all over the world and how this magic influences your personality and the ways you interact with the world, this book is divided in three main parts, which will guide you in a deep journey to discover your inner self. In part 1, "A Guide to the Traditional Odus," you'll discover all the main traditional aspects of practicing Odus, such as the meaning of the sixteen Odus that reveal themselves during African divination and their fortune-telling aspects. You'll also learn what *ebos* (magical rituals defined by each Odu) are and how these magical offerings work as spiritual medicines on the body and the soul, as well as the difference between the most common African ways to foresee the future.

In the second part, "Discovering the Odus in Your Orisha Birth Chart," you'll learn in detail all the techniques to create and assess a full Orisha birth chart. You'll learn how to calculate and interpret the six major houses and the four minor houses in their simple and complete forms. You'll also learn how to identify and interpret emotional behavioral styles based on Odu archetypes and will look at real-life examples to contextualize each of the sixteen main Odus for all the major and minor houses and will understand the differences between Odu interpretations in African oracles and birth charts, combining its outer and inner world influences.

In part 3, "Awakening Your Better Self," we'll set aside the practical aspects of African numerology and look into the emotional and subjective aspects of the Odus and how they influence your personality. By looking inside yourself, you'll learn how to understand and neutralize the Odus' negative aspects and how to potentialize their positive aspects in your day-to-day life. Also, with real-life examples, we'll find out how working to increase self-awareness in both aspects of the Odus can be used to transform the way you relate with people and transform the reality around you. We'll also take a brief look at other forms of applying African numerology, such as Odu charts for relationships and business, and how these tools can be used to help you achieve your goals and live a more complete and harmonious life.

At the end of the book, as a way of thanking you for your trust and confidence, you'll find instructions to get your own, free, and complete Orisha Birth Chart, interpreted by me and especially made for you.

Are you ready? Our soul journey begins now!

A Quick Word about Orishas and Odus

From now on we'll dive deeply into African spirituality: the ways it survived slavery in the Americas and how its concepts relate to our modern lives so we can evolve and improve ourselves with the Orishas' blessings. With that in mind, and to get the best from this book, two concepts must be explained before we begin: the Orishas and the Odus.

Who Are the Orishas?

The Orishas are deified ancestors who represent the forces of nature and are manifestations of these forces. Just like the forces to which they are related, the Orishas are present all the time, everywhere. As personified deities, the Orishas are close to humans and feel and act like us: they love, pray, eat, fight, appease, and advise. In addition, each Orisha has its own symbols and particular colors and requires its own specific prayers and offerings. Through making these prayers and offerings, we can receive their guidance and blessing.

It is said that, in Africa, more than 401 different Orishas were worshipped all over the continent, in each country or region. When Africans were enslaved and brought to the New World, they carried with them, to the various countries of the African diaspora, their spiritual practices and Orishas. These hundreds of deities were grouped into about sixteen Orisha families, each with its own characteristics and energies.

Besides ruling the world and the forces of nature, the Orishas have individual relationships with each of us, as every person is ruled by a particular Orisha called the head father or head mother. As we will see in the following chapters, the correct identification of this personal Orisha can be done only through the cowrie shell divination, performed by a *Babalosha* (male priest) or *Iyalosha* (female priestess) rightfully prepared for the use and interpretation of this oracle, which also represents the speech of the Orisha and provides guidance for the future.

What Are the Odus?

Imagine that you have decided to take a holiday trip, and there are sixteen main roads to reach your destination. On some of these roads the sun shines on green fields; on others, there are scary thunderstorms. There are still others that have a fine drizzle, but the landscape is enchanting, and it is worth getting a little wet to enjoy it.

Now also imagine that these roads are interconnected, creating new possible paths. When you start your trip, you follow a certain route that you have decided on and planned, but during the journey, you see a sign indicating a tourist spot that interests you, or you have a flat tire, or you decide to take a detour to have a snack. Each alteration in the original path brings you new travel options, new landscapes, and new challenges, and as time goes on, even if your destination remains the same, you have countless experiences that you never would have considered or anticipated simply because you decided to change the original itinerary of your trip.

In life and in the way we live our lives, the Odus are these roads, serving as possible ways for you to develop your best abilities and experience the pains and delights of living. Using another analogy, each Odu is a range of life possibilities, positive and negative events, mistakes and successes that everyone can go through during their journey on Earth. During a consultation with cowrie shells, the shells indicate one of the sixteen main Odus—the destiny roads where the Orishas come and go from Orun (the African heaven) to Aiye (Earth), receiving our offerings, granting us their blessings, and interacting with their devotees.

. . . .

Our lives are formed by a set of these Odus, by their intersections, and by the combination of these possibilities.

Further on, we'll understand in more detail how the Orishas and Odus relate to our day-to-day lives. For now, it's important to remember that these deities (Orishas) and their roads (Odus) can represent two universes at the same time: our *inner world* (who we are, what we think and do, and how we relate to all things around us) and the *outer world* (the external energies that, for better or for worse, influence our lives and interfere in the situations we live).

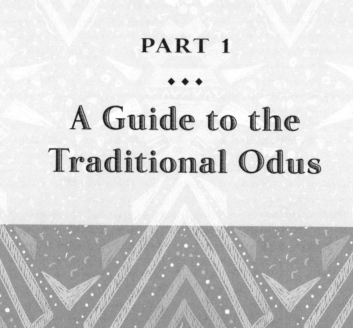

PART 1

• • •

A Guide to the Traditional Odus

3

Getting to Know the Odus

From a spiritual point of view, the Odus are the signs of Ifa, the African god of wisdom, identified and interpreted from the open and closed positions of the cowrie shells (see figure 1) during a consultation using cowrie shell divination, also called *merindilogun* divination, or with an Opelê Ifá—the traditional oracle of the Yoruba priests, a divination chain made of a string of eight opele seedpod halves.

It is through them that the Orishas and all spiritual energies communicate with us and influence our destiny, and through them Eshu, the African god of communication and movement, receives our offer-

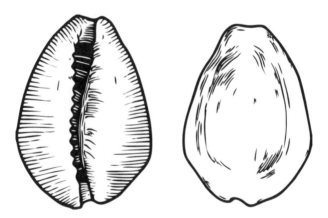

Fig. 1. On the left is the open side of the cowrie shell, with the natural slit; on the right is the closed side of the shell. This side is always considered closed even when the shell is perforated, either accidentally or deliberately.

ings and takes them to all other gods and goddesses, bringing their blessings. In his book *Mitologia dos Orixás* (2001), professor and researcher Reginaldo Prandi presents a traditional myth that explains it.

In remote times the gods went hungry.
Sometimes, for long periods,
they didn't get enough food.
The gods increasingly became indisposed with each
*   other*
and amazing wars fought among themselves.

Without the protection of the gods, misfortune had
*   befallen the Earth and men lived sick, poor,*
*   unhappy.*
One day Eshu took the road and went looking for a
*   solution.*

Eshu went to a place where there were palm trees
and got sixteen coconuts from monkeys.
Eshu thought and thought, but did not understand
what to do with them.
The monkeys then said to him:
—Eshu, you don't know what to do
with sixteen palm coconuts?
Go around the world
and in each place ask
what do these palm coconuts mean.
You must go to sixteen places to find out what they
*   mean*
those sixteen palm coconuts.
In each of these places you will collect sixteen Odus.
You will collect sixteen stories, sixteen oracles.
Each story has its wisdom,
Advice that can help men.
Join the Odus

and at the end of a year, you will have learned enough.
You will learn sixteen times sixteen Odus.

The gods then taught the new knowledge
to their descendants, men.
The men then got to know every day
the designs of the gods and the events to come.

As we see in the verses of this myth, Eshu went around the world to save men and gods, learning "sixteen times sixteen Odus." That is why Odus are divided into two groups, totaling 256 combinations: the main 16, called Odu Meji; and the 240 secondary ones, called Omo Odu. The names of the 16 main Odus are:

1. Okaran
2. Ejioko
3. Eta-Ogunda or Ogunda
4. Iorossun
5. Oshe
6. Obara
7. Odi
8. Ejiogbe or Ejionile
9. Ossa
10. Ofun
11. Owarin
12. Ejilaxebora
13. Ojiologbon or Ejiologbon
14. Ika
15. Obeogunda
16. Alafia

Each of the 256 Odus is represented by innumerable myths and legends; these stories provide advice and guidance from the Orishas for the different situations of spiritual and daily life. By correctly interpreting the messages contained in these myths, priests identify the situations that transpire the lives of those who seek them and point out the energies that are interfering in both positive and negative ways.

By identifying the situation, an Orisha priest also diagnoses the origin of the problem, indicating the solution to be carried out for each situation. It may be that the querent needs to have a change in attitude or needs to correct some choices that the querent made in relation to life and the people around him or her. The querent may also need to perform magical rituals and make offerings to the Orishas; these offerings are commonly called *ebos*.

EBOS: FOOD THAT PLEASES THE GODS

The word *ebo*, of Yoruba origin, means "food offering." It originates in the verb *bo*, "to feed," and it can summarize in a single word the greatest meaning of the Orishas' faith: feeding the body, mind, and spirit with the different forces of nature. It is not by chance that the basis of Candomblé, Batuque, Umbanda, and Kimbanda—the main religions of African origin practiced in Brazil—is the offering of votive foods.

Brazilian cuisine—especially the foods that originated in Bahia and throughout the northeast of the country, where the Orisha religions started—has its origins in the slave quarters and markets and represents very well this intimate connection that the gods and human beings have with each other. In *Comida de Santo que Se Come** (Ribeiro 2018), by chef Carlos Ribeiro with Vilson Caetano de Sousa Jr., professor and anthropological researcher of Afro-Brazilian food and culture, Vilson describes well this relationship between food and religion.

> In religions of African origin, food is understood as strength, gift, energy present in the grains, roots, leaves and fruits that spring from the earth. Food is the strength that feeds the ancestors, and at the same time the means through which the community reaches the highest degree of intimacy with the sacred through consummation. . . .
>
> In the kitchens of the temples, grains, roots, leaves, fruits, vegetables, meat and drinks receive special treatment, and through the words of enchantment they become true ancestral bodies that must be consumed by the communities. . . .
>
> In religions of African origin there are foods from sacrifices

---

*In English, "Sacred Food to Be Eaten"; no foreign editions are so far available.

[animals], called foods of ejé, and dry foods, those made from cereals, tubers, legumes, leaves and fruits.

Much more than just nourishment, food is what brings a community closer, unites it, and reconnects it to the deities, who, like their devotees, share it with them, uniting people and gods. Here is one of the biggest secrets brought by enslaved Africans to Brazil and consolidated in spiritual traditions: food nourishes, strengthens, rejoices, and heals.

It is interesting to observe that, for an offer to be accepted, the one who offers it must always, necessarily, eat the first part after giving it, in communion to Eshu, the divine communicator. Still on this issue, the babalawo Adilson Antônio Martins (African name Ifaleke Aráilé Obi), in his book *O Jogo de Búzios por Odu** (2012), tells us a little about African culture, in which the physical and the spiritual are always intertwined.

A tree leaf does not fall without a spiritual predetermination or a religious background. . . . The superior forces are always asked to solve everyday problems and, whatever the religion of choice of the individual, the practice of magic is always adopted in the search for its solutions, even if this practice is veiled or masked under other names.

That is why, for all problems or dangers identified during consultation with cowrie shells, Odu myths and meanings will indicate a magical ritual—an ebo—to achieve the desired solution; the ebo is a true spiritual medicine. In the same way, for any positive and satisfactory situation and to keep the Odus in our lives, Odus will also indicate ebos that will serve as a gift and pleasure to the deities, strengthening the communion between ourselves and the spiritual energies and, therefore, attracting and potentializing their influences on our lives, allowing

---

*In English, "Cowrie Shell Divination Using the Odus"; no foreign editions are so far available.

things to go the way we want and multiply according to the indications contained in each Odu.

An important warning, however, is that just as all Orishas are related to one or more Odus, all ebos are also linked to the Odus' myths and symbolisms. Because they are spiritual remedies, no ebo should be performed without first consulting the Odus; otherwise, the wrong ebo may be performed with a negative instead of a positive consequence. Paracelsus said in the mid-sixteenth century that "the difference between the remedy and the poison is the dose." It may seem strange to think this way until we understand that ebos often have positive and objective aspects of enhancing a certain energy or situation in our lives, and we may unwittingly enhance an energy we would rather diminish. We must remember that the basic principle of human existence is balance.

Specifically on the symbolism of spiritual balance in relation to the initiation rites and the identification of the individual within the scope of the Orisha temples (called *terreiros*), the anthropologists José Flávio Pessoa de Barros and Maria Lina Leão Teixeira (1989), in their article "O Código do Corpo: Inscrições e Marcas dos Orixás" (The Body Code: Inscriptions and Marks of the Orishas), affirm that

> basic beliefs and feelings in the Terreiros' social life are associated and are sent to the human body, constituting a set of representations that go beyond the biological characteristics inherent to the human being. This appreciation can still be explained by the fact that the human body is the vehicle of communication with the gods, forces of nature, which, through ritual possession, are embodied in their "horses" or mediums.

We realized that in the course of initiation the notion of balance is identified with that of health. The valorization of balance and order leads to the requirement that all animals used in the sacrifices that accompany the initiation rituals are perfect and in accordance with others of their kind, thus showing that such notions are synonymous with health, which is considered to be priceless and typical of nature.

Candomblé supporters believe that health and well-being will only be restored after the fulfillment of certain ritual obligations that formalize and, from then on, balance the relationship between the individual and the Orisha.

In Candomblé we do not find the dualism of body and soul. On the contrary, we perceive as Lépine (1983, 29) that the "soul has something material and the body something spiritual," which is in accordance with the idea that everything that exists in the physical world is also found in the "orum," supernatural world, and vice versa.

As we saw earlier, each Odu and the hundreds of possible combinations among them brings with it positive and negative aspects, and all humans are subject to both aspects of each Odu. For our lives to be harmonious and for us to evolve, our inner world needs to be in balance with the influences of the outer world.

As I explain in my book *Sacred Leaves: A Magical Guide to Orisha Herbal Witchcraft* (Llewellyn Worldwide, 2022) about the use of herbal baths, when performing a ritual for achieving wealth and prosperity—for example, even if the initial objective is to attract financial resources—there is no point in using the ingredients solely to achieve that goal without first preparing to manage the money. Uniting all the specific ingredients to a single objective can turn the ritual into an energy bomb, with the result that we attract or repel an energy that is not exactly what we need to achieve balance, and this energy, instead of healing the pain or potentiating the blessing, performs the opposite effect. In the prosperity example, what is missing may not be the money itself: the money may come and go without us realizing how our behavior is affecting its flow. In the case of someone seeking love through a love ritual, the person may not be missing someone to love: it may be that the person is loved but demands so much without giving anything in return that he or she unconsciously pushes people away. In regard to health, what affects us is not always the disease: we have a healthy body, but the anxieties and fears the soul has been unable to process express themselves physically through ailments.

The key to your personal revolution, to truly transform your life, is precisely to understand how each of the energies from the outside can be balanced with the energies from within, whether through conscious work on your birth Odus or through magical rituals.

The blessings of the Orishas come to those who recognize themselves as a unique being in the universe and everything in the universe is energy in balance.

4

The Sixteen Odus

As we have just learned, everything in the universe must be in balance, and therefore, if there is something that says yes, we must necessarily also have its complementary opposite that says no. If there is light, there must also be darkness. If there is a force that attracts, there must also be one that repels. The same happens with the sixteen Odus.

It is true that each Odu is balanced in itself, bringing positive and negative aspects in its own *itans*—the traditional myths and legends. This constant balance, however, goes much further: of the sixteen main Odus, we'll have eight considered male and another eight considered female, each being represented in cowrie shell divination by their respective shapes, male and female. In the same way, each main Odu is represented by a geomantic sign formed by four rows containing one or two shells each, which then form one or two vertical lines. These shapes can be traced or marked with various elements during the Orisha magical rituals, such as vegetable powder, seeds, sand, or cowrie shells (see figure 2). (Note: *The number of vertical lines in these signs has nothing to do with the respective Odu number that identifies it in African numerology or that is read by priests during a consultation of the oracle.*) There are eight different geomantic signs distributed among the sixteen Odus, facing upward or downward, completing the sixteen main signs that will balance the male and female energies of the Odus.

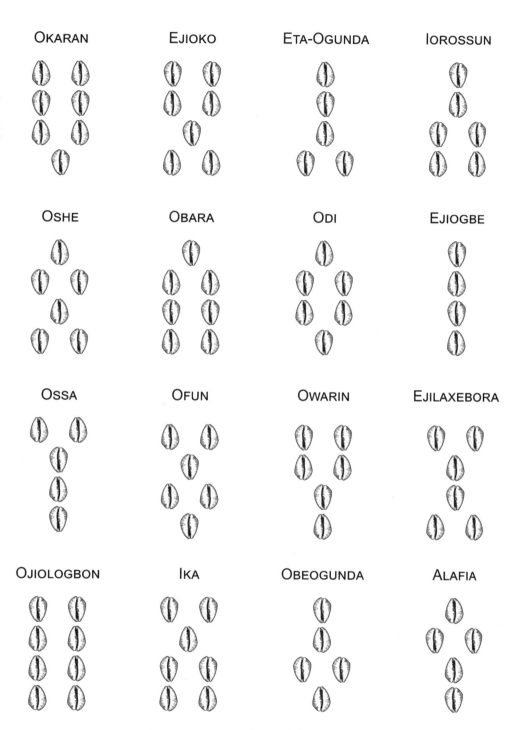

Fig. 2. The sixteen main Odus and their geomantic signs

Next, we'll see the general descriptions of the domains and predicates of each main Odu, its symbol, and the corresponding number of open shells that are identified each time the cowrie shells are thrown on a table or a towel during a consultation. It is from this reference number that, in the following chapters, you'll learn how to calculate the birth Odus and build the Orisha birth chart. For now, let's just stick to the meaning of these Odus in their interpretation in African oracles.

. . . .

A Warning before Continuing about Interpreting the Odus

It is essential to emphasize that the following explanations are only generalizations about the interpretation of each of the sixteen main Odus. As we have seen earlier, their specific meanings are revealed through the myths of their 256 possible combinations. For this reason, even though knowledge about their meanings is fundamental for a good and correct interpretation of the Orisha birth chart, consultation with Odus as a divinatory and oracular method can only be performed by priests and priestesses rightfully initiated in its mysteries, which requires years of theoretical and religious study. To try to work with with Orisha oracles without passing through the proper initiation rituals will not only be ineffective but also is disrespectful to the deities—especially to Eshu, god of communication, the one who both gratifies the loyal and true and punishes liars without mercy.

. . . .

OKARAN

Represented by one open shell and fifteen closed shells, Okaran is par excellence the path of the Orisha Eshu and, like him, deals with the contradictions and contrasts that can either crown or condemn the one to whom this Odu presents itself. Precisely for this reason, it is an extremely delicate Odu, and whenever Okaran comes during an oracle divination, regardless of whether in its positive or negative aspect, the

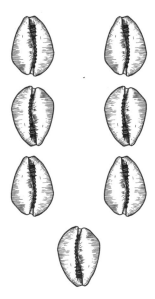

priest must immediately pause the service and offer three portions of freshwater to the street, a symbolic gesture that calms the entrance of the temple and the paths of those who pass through it.

In its positive aspect, Okaran indicates total protection and victory guaranteed by the Orishas, after all the ebos designated in the consultation are strictly followed to neutralize the influence of any threats along the way, allowing Eshu to act in the search for victory. Not fulfilling this request for ebos can reverse Okaran's influence and awaken the fury of the Orishas.

On the negative side, Okaran can be terrible and point to all kinds of imminent and immediate dangers, life risks, robberies, betrayals, and attacks by witchcraft. It also indicates the fanaticism (especially religious) that prevents rational thinking.

EJIOKO

Represented by two open shells and fourteen closed shells, Ejioko is the Odu of creativity, multiplication, and novelties. Ejioko is the spiritual path for the Orishas Ogun, Ibeyi, and Babaluaiye; in their positive aspect, they indicate unions, social gatherings, and marriages. It is

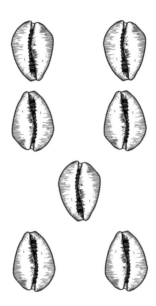

Ejioko who, along with the Odus Oshe and Ossa, governs pregnancies and, specifically, fetuses; Ejioko also represents everything that is swollen and rounded. It is he who commands everything that is born and begins, the emergence of new situations, ideas, and opportunities for transformation.

In Ejioko's negative aspect, the Odu points to the innocence and naïveté that can make a person vulnerable to harm. It can also lead to disputes for assets between partners and for inheritance within a family, separation of a couple, and risky pregnancy under the influence of Egbe Abiku—an African secret society of spiritual child entities. It represents everything that is rounded. When this Odu presents itself repeatedly at the same consultation, it demands care and offerings to the Orisha Ogun to rule out the risk of theft, encounters with the police, and court cases.

In some traditions, Ejioko is also the Odu that gives way to Orisha Aje Salunga, goddess of material wealth, abundance of resources, and financial prosperity. This Orisha is linked to the principles of the creation of the world; in some myths, she is mother, and in others, sister of Olokun, the deep ocean. Aje Salunga is worshipped in Brazil and is otherwise little known.

OGUNDA

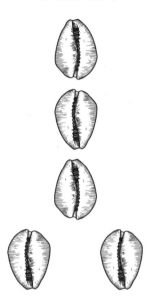

Represented by three open shells and thirteen closed shells, Ogunda is the Odu of war, strategy, progress, and persistence. Like Ejioko, Odu Ogunda is also the path of the Orishas Ogun and Babaluaiye. It is an essentially male Odu, in contrast to Odu Ossa, discussed later. Its symbols are the knife, the sword, and the machete, indicating its dominance over all metals and over everything that cuts or separates; likewise, it is Odu Ogunda who rules the phallus, testicles, and erections.

In its positive aspect, this Odu represents the sword of divine law. As an Odu of battles, still in its positive aspect, Ogunda indicates sovereign victory through planning and patience to carry out what is needed at the right time. It announces the improvement of situations through effort and advises that persistence and personal trust are the keys to achieve the goals.

The negative aspect of this Odu is considered extremely dangerous, precisely because of the symbolism it carries. Ogunda warns of theft, involvement in melees and firearm fights, prison, court cases, all kinds of addictions, and venereal diseases. Negative Ogunda governs lies, deceit, and, in some cases, death.

IOROSSUN

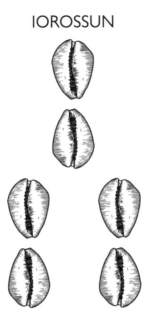

Represented by four open shells and twelve closed shells, Iorossun is the Odu of language, written communication, and logical and theoretical reasoning. Iorossun is also the Odu of family relationships, especially parental relationships. It is the path of the Orishas Yemaya, Oshossi, and Ori, who is the spiritual head.

In its positive aspect, Iorossun indicates the balance of reason over emotion, eloquence in words, and great capacity for learning and spiritual wisdom. It may indicate a destiny to join a priesthood. As the main Odu representative of balance in all aspects of life, Iorossun usually foreshadows average achievements but which meet all needs.

Iorossun's negative aspect indicates lack of financial resources, talk and gossip, falsehoods and lies, and intrigues. It brings influences from the Orishas Oya and Nanna, in addition to a great relationship with Egun, the Orisha of ancestral spirits, and Iku, the Orisha of death. In such cases, it is essential to observe the paths of this Odu so that the rituals necessary for Ori's rebalancing are carried out; after all, *the head carries the body*. Because of Iorossun's relationship with Iku, in some cases (observing other Odus in combination with it), this Odu deals with bloodshed caused by violence or illness, especially for women.

OSHE

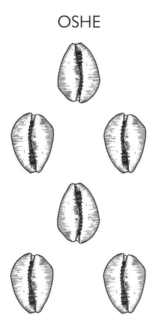

Represented by five open shells and eleven closed shells, Oshe is the Odu of beauty, seduction, feminine mysteries, intuition, and spirituality through magical practice. It is the path for Orisha Oshun, the goddess of freshwaters and gold, and, in some cases, of Babaluaiye, the lord of Earth.

When in its positive influence, Oshe brings great achievements: personal recognition, material and symbolic wealth, love (although it does not represent the continuation of relationships), pregnancy, and creative inspiration.

In its negative aspect, this Odu brings with it the hidden strength of witchcraft through the influence of Ìyá Mi, bird-women who keep the secret of life and death in their magical womb. It is a dangerous Odu, which can indicate all kinds of betrayals and losses, including that of personal prestige through defamation, envy, falsehood, and waste.

In any of its aspects, it is a very demanding Odu, only accepting what is beautiful, well taken care of, done with care, and, preferably, expensive. Odu Oshe's values are much more related to what things cost—and, therefore, can be flaunted and displayed—than to what they subjectively symbolize.

OBARA

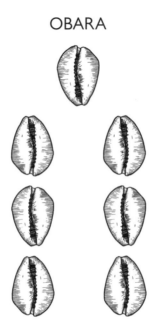

Represented by six open shells and ten closed shells, Obara is the Odu of prosperity, joy, and material conquests; it is the path of the Orishas Oshossi, Shango, and Logunede.

Obara is essentially a positive Odu, and even in its reverse aspect, it is not a harbinger of defeat or absolute loss. There are always alternatives for material recovery, as long as the rituals indicated by its myths are strictly fulfilled and the querent becomes aware of the real world instead of daydreams and fantasies, as this Odu always indicates idealization over reality.

Obara also represents friendships and social relationships, the ease of communicating, extroversion, and the pleasures of the world. In this way, it is a path that leads to expansion in all directions, such as increased money and inheritances. It also relates to bureaucracies and documents.

When in its negative vibration, Odu Obara indicates risks of theft or money losses, financial mismanagement, poor personal planning, avarice, and exacerbated pride. Being an Odu given to pleasures, it can sometimes deal with sexual excesses and deviations, adultery, and male homosexuality.

ODI

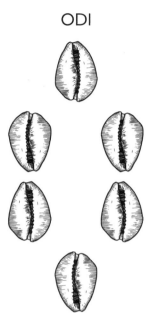

Represented by seven open shells and nine closed shells, Odi is one of the most complex and difficult Odus to treat. Just as Obara is essentially positive, Odi is essentially negative, even when in *ire*—the positive aspect of Odus. Odi is the path of difficulty, losses in general, diseases of the body, and efforts that are not satisfactorily rewarded. It also represents overcoming obstacles through struggle. In this Odu, all Orishas can present themselves, depending on their combinations with the other Odus during the consultation; still, Odi receives direct influence from Eshu, Ogun, and Babaluaiye. The name of this Odu should never be pronounced at night, as the mere mention of it can attract the most negative aspect of the querent's energy.

In its positive aspect, Odi always bears average messages, indicating that the situation in question will be resolved "in the best possible way," which generally means "not necessarily in the expected or desired way."

In its negative aspect, Odi always answers "absolutely not" to any question. Its negative responses can also indicate witchcraft, moral and financial damage, possession by evil spirits, and closed paths. In these negative situations, the querent must urgently engage in the indicated rituals.

EJIOGBE

Represented by eight open shells and eight closed shells, Ejiogbe is the Odu of duality; it represents the balance between light and shadows. All other Odus were born from Ejiogbe, except for Ofun, the oldest, from whom Ejiogbe originates. These two Odus—Ejiogbe and Ofun—are the paths of creation and are, therefore, represented by Oshoguian, the "Young Oshala,"* and Obatala, the "Elder Oshala," respectively. Ejiogbe is also the path of Shango Aiyra, the Orisha who rescued Obatala from unjust imprisonment.

In contrast to Odu Odi, when Ejiogbe says that *everything will happen as far as possible,* this Odu, in its positive aspect, means that *everything will be better than imagined.* For this reason, it is the bearer of the best answers to everything and indicates absolute and lasting independence and achievement in all areas of life, including intellectual and financial.

In its negative aspect, called Ejionile, it is the Odu of doubt and points to betrayals, persecutions of all kinds, gambling and addictions,

---

*Oshala is a common name given to all male Orishas of Creation.

stubbornness, aggressiveness (especially in words), judicial problems, envy that seriously damages, doubts, and moral quandaries. In such cases, along with the recommended rituals, one must take care of both Ejionile and Ori, the head Odu.

OSSA

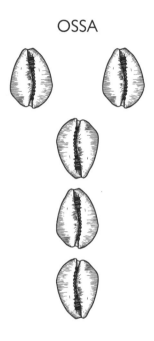

Represented by nine open shells and seven closed shells, Ossa is the Odu of intensity, dynamism, independence, and courage. In opposition to Odu Ogunda, which is essentially masculine, Odu Ossa is fundamentally feminine, and all its predicates are related to women or involve them in the situations that it foreshadows. It is considered a fire Odu, complementary to Iorossun, a water Odu: it is even right to say that just as Iorossun is the water that calms Ossa, it is Ossa the fire that boils and awakens Iorossun's fury. For this complementarity, the Odu Ossa is also the path of the Orishas Oya, Yemaya, Nanna, and Ori.

In its positive aspects, Ossa brings victory and material progress, personal and financial independence, intuition and prophetic dreams. When dealing with business, it predicts the opening of new companies or the separation of companies so that one follows an individual path.

In love, it is the Odu of passions, of female sexuality, also governing female genitals and menstruation.

In its negative aspects, Ossa brings great influence from Egun and the ancestors, evil magic and witchcraft, persecutions and attacks by women against the querent, abortions, falsehoods, and breaking of religious laws and taboos.

OFUN

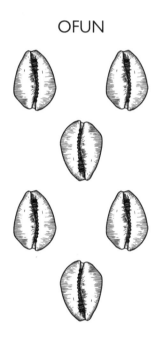

Represented by ten open shells and six closed shells, Ofun was the first Odu to be created, par excellence, being the path of Obatala, the oldest of the Orishas and the father of creation. It is from Ofun that the Odu Ejiogbe is born, which then gives rise to all the other Odus.

It is considered the Odu of wisdom, the one who knows and consequently hides or reveals all secrets, including those of life and death. It represents all the elderly and elders' matters, all that lasts for a long time or forever, all that is old. For this reason, in its positive aspect, it ensures victory over any obstacle, even if it also means that the achievement will take time to be realized. It governs the eloquence of spoken words, the conviction by argument and rhetoric, credibility and good character. Together with Odu Ossa, Ofun controls menstruation and female bleeding.

The reverse of Odu Ofun, however, brings persecution and disturbance, lack of resources and the means to obtain them, injustice and condemnation, demoralization and the loss of public respect. It is necessary, above all, to consider Ofun's antiquity in all that it predicts: what Ofun brings is forever and what it takes away is gone forever, too.

OWARIN

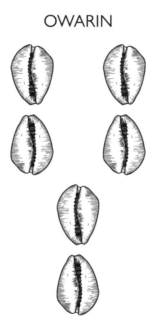

Represented by eleven open shells and five closed shells, Owarin is the Odu of contrasts, ruled by the Orishas Eshu, Oya, and Ogun. Just as Odu Ofun is responsible for everything that lingers, Owarin is the Odu that governs immediacy, speed, and urgency.

In its positive aspect, Owarin foreshadows extremely favorable outcomes and is considered the Odu of good luck; it indicates that the solution to a problem will happen soon. Owarin brings financial growth to those who attend to it; however, the growth does not continue because, like the fire that burns and consumes, Owarin acts quickly but the results don't last. It governs material wealth, luck in gambling, financial ventures, and social or economic partnerships between two people.

In the negative aspect of this Odu, its influence is proportional to its intensity. With this, as well as guaranteeing blessings quickly and agiley, it also indicates loss, defeat, bankruptcy, and, in some cases, according to its combinations, sudden death without warning. In this same way, it is called the Odu of ingratitude, and, if not taken care of through ebos, Owarin makes a person take responsibility for what was done, by that person and all others involved in the situation.

EJILAXEBORA

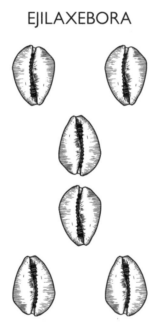

Represented by twelve open shells and four closed shells, Ejilaxebora is the Odu of royalty and likes what is showy and opulent and abundant; it is responsible for material prosperity. It also deals with sexual relations as a means of pleasure, dilettante excesses, and resignation instead of facing the efforts to achieve what is needed.

For the same reason, it is an administrative Odu: it regulates and commands, indicating who or what should perform deeds and make efforts but does not perform those functions itself. It is the Odu of justice and truth, bureaucracy, politics, contracts, and everything that involves negotiations of all kinds. Under the command of Orisha Shango, Ejilaxebora is also the Odu that governs unions, societies, pacts, and commitments of any kind.

However, Ejilaxebora constantly flirts with tyranny, and its negative aspect predicts defeat in judicial matters, imprisonment, financial loss, lying, and difficulties of all kinds that are aggravated by objective or symbolic bureaucracy. This Odu is on the border between the physical and the spiritual worlds and, like Odu Ogunda, is related to depression and suicidal tendencies.

OJIOLOGBON

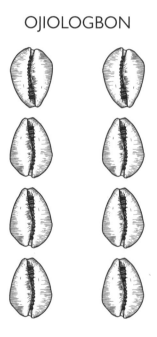

Represented by thirteen open shells and three closed shells, Ojiologbon, also called Ologbon or Eji Ologbon, is perhaps the most feared Odu of the main sixteen. Ojiologbon is the path of the Orishas Nanna, Babaluaiye, Egun, and Iku and represents death, purely and simply, be it physical or symbolic. In this way, even in its positive aspect, Ojiologbon is not an Odu that foreshadows good because it will always indicate closure, the end, the exhaustion of what is being asked about. As Babalawo

Adilson Antônio Martins (2013) says, "Eji Ologbon is the night, the reverse of the day; it is death, the reverse of life."

Still, in its positive aspect, this Odu represents the end of suffering, the closure of an uncomfortable issue, even though this ending does not indicate the emergence of happiness. On the contrary, it is a neutral path that symbolizes inefficiency, conformation and resignation, saying that "what had no solution is now solved."

In its negative aspect, Ojiologbon is literal and most often points to death from old age or illness. Depending on the combination, it can indicate the end of relationships, inactivity and inertia, or the definitive closure of any issue.

IKA

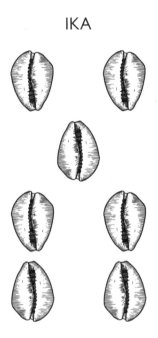

Represented by fourteen open shells and two closed shells, Ika is the Odu of rebirth, of transformation, of what is long and continuous. It is the path for the Orishas Oshumare, Ossain, Iroko, and sometimes Ibeyi. Ika is intense and dynamic, bordering on exaggeration and excessiveness. Symbolically, Odu Ika is a powder keg that is about to explode, assuming any risks for renovation, even if destruction is inevitable.

As a positive aspect, this Odu brings good surprises and good news. It also brings sudden changes in the status quo without warning and with no preparation, requiring attention. Under the leadership of Orisha Oshumare, Ika deals with financial growth, fortune through inheritances and contracts, obtaining favors and benefits through gifts and thanks.

In contrast, its negative aspect invites all kinds of violence and aggression: sexual crimes and violence with firearms and knives. It also deals with riots, crowds, complications with the police, wickedness, abuse of power, and marital betrayal. Together with the Odus Ossa and Ofun, it governs hemorrhages and abortions. If a pregnant woman seeking a consultation receives this Odu, she requires urgent care.

OBEOGUNDA

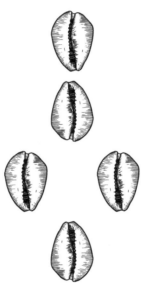

Represented by fifteen open shells and one closed shell, Obeogunda is the Odu of heroic excesses, courage and bravery that disregard common sense, breaking boundaries (or the complete absence of them), sexual impulse that is either released or transmuted in violence, disobedience to the rules, and lack of discipline. It is the path for the Orishas

Obba, Iyewá, Yemaya, and Ogun: both their positive and negative aspects are at the extremes. There are no middle terms for Obeogunda's foreshadowing.

On the positive side, Obeogunda speaks of conquering and dominating any situation, of overwhelming passions, of social and political influence, of the arrival of a powerful aid that will solve any problems. In this sense, it is always important to check the rituals needed to balance its influence, ensuring that the blessings obtained are consistent and lasting.

On the negative side, it deals with amorous adventures that end badly, disappointment and disbursement, threatening postures that control by fear and threats, abuses of all kinds, uncontrollable jealousies, sexual violence resulting from jealousy, and, ultimately, rape and murder.

ALAFIA

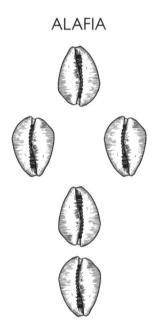

Represented by sixteen open shells, Alafia is the Odu of absolute peace, of the primordial triumph that voids the need for any desire or goal: if you have everything you need, you are no longer allowed to seek anything. Alafia—which represents alpha and omega, simultaneously the beginning and the ending—is the path of the Orishas Orunmila (god of the heavens, an unattainable creator and, therefore, inert) and Elegbara (the primordial epithet of Eshu, the god of movement, duality, and perpetual dynamism). It is the Odu of utopia, the furthest horizon to be conquered that, with each step forward, continually recedes.

In its positive aspect, Alafia points to peace, rest after the effort that led to a conquest, an artistic vocation, wisdom, the love and affection shared among peers, profits and inheritances, and complete health and happiness attained through order.

In its negative aspect, however, Alafia contradicts everything and transforms itself into chaos and disorder, unrest that unbalances the emotions and brings psychiatric disorders, illusion, and lies. Its negative aspect is in the domain of instincts and biological needs that lack reason.

5

Cowrie Shell Divination

The Orishas' Voices

The challenges of the twenty-first century make life seem faster every day, giving the impression that there is never enough time to fulfill all commitments, even less to accomplish what truly pleases you, right? What is most intriguing, perhaps, is that this crazy routine seems to happen in all phases of life. It doesn't matter if you are twenty, thirty, or fifty years old. For many of us, after we left adolescence and assumed the responsibilities of adult life, it seems that we have not had the opportunity to look inside ourselves, to listen to our hearts and take care of our interior garden with the same tranquillity and dedication that was possible in our youth.

I speak from experience: I started working formally as soon as I turned sixteen, as an intern in the technology department of my high school. A few months before I turned eighteen, I got on a bus loaded with all my luggage, left a city of two hundred thousand inhabitants, and traveled to a stone jungle called São Paulo, where I shared an apartment with friends and dedicated practically all my time to my college studies and to building the first steps of my career in computer science so that I could pay the bills of early adulthood. Step by step, I garnered small promotions in my job until, five years later and with a well-structured career, the first major demands and professional commitments of my job arose, with business trips and opportunities for financial growth.

It felt like the fulfillment of a big dream, and at that moment, I felt like I had reached the top of the big mountain I had decided to climb when I was a teenager. I felt complete, proud of myself, and deserving of all my laurels; after all, I had worked tirelessly for many years to get there.

Little did I know that upon reaching those first goals, new and bigger goals would appear immediately afterward and, with them, new and even greater demands. Faced with these new challenges, the taste of victory that I had experienced a few months earlier was beginning to lose its savor. At that point in my life, I was already seeking my second college degree (truth be told, I never completed the first one). I had left the apartment I shared with colleagues to live alone, in another neighborhood in the city, and my social circle was completely different from when I first arrived in town.

I looked around, observing the life, routines, and stories told by my friends at the time, and realized that the same thing had happened to all of us. We had big dreams and plans, and with each passing year, it seemed like there was less time to achieve them. The days were filled with routine: completing studies and studying further, building a good marriage, raising children, looking after the house, and paying the mortgage and bills. With each day we all had to face new choices, new decisions, and new doubts. Well, I think you know what I mean, right?

Amid all this, many times I felt at a crossroads, not knowing which way to choose—as I bet you have, too. How many times did I look at the sky and ask, *My gods, what is my destiny?* How many times, with a lump in my throat, did I eagerly wish to hear one divine word that would indicate how to move forward and, even with so many challenges, how to find a moment of lasting peace and happiness.

Until one day I finally heard this voice! The first time I went to consult on a cowrie shell divination, I could clearly feel the presence of the Orishas. It was like listening to them beside me, telling my heart everything that should be done from then on. They called me, they spoke with me and to me, they guided me regarding life's ifs and if-nots so that I could finally choose the best way to go without being at the mercy of events. They taught me to become a better person on a daily basis, and when the world's pains and dangers approached, they reached out to me and performed their magic to protect against the world's evil and against my own inner demons.

When I heard the voice of the Orishas for the first time, I realized that I had a life mission and that I should turn that mission into purpose: to take the word of the Orishas to all people who desired to hear the word, who sought answers and were willing to listen. For all these reasons, I became a Babalosha and dedicated my life from then on to studying and understanding how that voice was heard and what messages it transmitted.

WHAT IS COWRIE SHELL DIVINATION, AFTER ALL?

Cowrie shell divination is the voice of the Orishas, through which, with the proper interpretation of the Odus to which these Orishas relate and the combinations between them, the Orisha priest or priestess (Babalosha or Iyalosha, also called *Iyalorisha*) interprets the message of the deities, be it of blessing or danger. It is also through these interpretations that it will be possible to identify which Orisha you're affiliated with as a spiritual father and mother, which other Orishas bless your spiritual life, and which energies of the universe are interfering in a positive or negative way so that you can reach your desires and goals.

Cowrie shell divination reveals your desires, your dreams and goals, the prospects for your future, the ways you can keep living a winning life, or the reasons why you have not yet reached what you wanted—whether you are responsible for those reasons, in which case the priest should provide guidance for behavioral changes or decision-making; or whether the reasons are external influences, in which case the priest should instruct you about magic rituals you need to perform. In both cases, especially based on Odus' interpretations, the priest identifies ways of correcting and solving problems, enhancing solutions, and healing all kinds of ills of the body and soul—health, career and work, personal evolution and challenges, love and relationships, and many other issues—through ebos.

Beyond how the divination is performed, it is necessary to understand exactly what the divination is and is not and can and cannot do.

The cowrie shell divination deals with the external energies and forces that are influencing your path at this moment of your life, presenting a snapshot of the world around you and the way it affects you.

This may seem like just a semantic issue, but it is important to understand that the future as we usually think of it, in the sense of facts that have not yet occurred and that are predetermined to appear in our lives by determination of some supernatural force, *does not exist!* We are free and thinking beings, endowed with analytical capacity and the power to make decisions, even though, many times, we decide not to take any action and let situations proceed according to the wishes of others.

Perhaps I am taking a great risk in saying this, but the truth is this: no oracle and no priest who is faithful to a serious spiritual tradition, whatever it may be, has the gift of foreseeing the future. Just as no one goes to the doctor and undergoes procedures to treat body ailments that do not yet exist, no one goes to the gods to remove what has not yet come into your life or to modify what is not yet known or that has not yet happened.

Can you see now the reason for the meditations indicated in the first chapter of the book? Can you understand the importance of taking on your life and deciding, consciously and truly, to take responsibility for your present?

In this sense, the cowrie shell divination unveils your present, identifies which energies are influencing your present moment in life, understands the reasons from the past that gave rise to it, and, through Orunmila's wisdom, informs what will be the results of present choices and attitudes in the future *if you do not change, if you do not take action in the face of these predictions.* Remember the story I told in chapter 1 about the woman who was persecuted at work and years later faced the same problems? The oracle unveiled her present, identified the origins of her difficulties, and indicated possible solutions, among them changing jobs. Did she change? No! Did she choose not to change? Yes! Whether consciously or unconsciously. And so the predictions were not fulfilled.

Once you understand this, you'll begin to understand the true magic of the Orishas, which is the multiplication of blessings through the dynamics of the *gift,* a concept developed by the French sociologist and anthropologist Marcel Mauss (1872–1950). About this, I excerpt several paragraphs from my book *The Sacred Leaves.*

> In a simplified way, the researcher states that all human relationships, physical or symbolic, are based on the dynamics of the gift: giving, receiving and giving back. In the article "The sociology of Marcel Mauss: Gift, symbolism and association," published in the *Revista Crítica de Ciências Sociais,* which discusses the social and political implications of Marcell Mauss's theory, the author says:
>
> The gift is present everywhere and is not just about isolated and discontinuous moments in reality. What circulates has several names: it's called money, car, furniture, clothes, but also smiles, kindness, words, hospitality, gifts, free services, among many others. . . . Differently from other animals, the human is characterized by the presence of the will, the pressure of the conscience of one on others, the communication of ideas, language, plastic and aesthetic arts, groups and religions, in a word, complements, of the "institutions that are the trait of our life in common." (Martins 2005)

Although Mauss's theory deals with practical issues in the relations between human societies, from his concept of gift it is possible to perceive the dynamics of the energies of which we speak: if I give in a negative way, I also receive negatively and repay equally; whereas if I do in a positive way, I receive positivism, and, therefore, I return positively.

Since all of this happens automatically, imagine the fantastic results that we could achieve using this same dynamic in a conscious way!

In African religions, this practice is taken even further: those who believe in the strength and power of the Orishas experience the gift almost daily, even when they are unaware of it. When we make our offerings in thanks for the blessings received, when we light a candle to strengthen the intentions of our rituals, when we praise our Orishas through songs and ritual dances . . . Anyway, any act dedicated to the Orishas is a gift that, due to the spiritual character of religious practice, gains two new components: magic and purpose.

In this way, we can say that any and all acts of devotion or ritual performed to the Orishas are, in themselves, an act of magic—after all, we believe that the strength and power of the Orishas are capable of producing inexplicable effects in our lives. At the same time, an act of magic is always guided by a motivation, by an objective: whoever makes a request, asks for something; whoever gives thanks, thanks for some result. Therefore, the practice of spirituality is based, precisely, on the union of these three aspects: conscience—I know what I am doing and I do it of my own free will; magic—I seek divine intervention to transform the energies of the ritual elements into supernatural results; and purpose—I have a specific goal for what I do.

However, to move forward, we need to remember a fundamental factor: none of these three aspects exempts us from taking responsibility for what we are looking for, for what we are doing from now until the desired result is achieved, and, especially, for what we'll do after conquering our desires or achieving our purpose. The continuous cycle of giving and receiving expands as we practice it throughout our life. We must be careful not to break the cycle if we are to live in harmony, happiness, and prosperity. By doing so we can elevate ourselves from mere resemblance to our creator, and we can become divine beings.

It is because we look at the past, present, and future in this way that, unlike other oracles, when consulting the cowrie shell divination, you do not need to ask any questions. Orunmila, along with Eshu, knows exactly what is going on in your heart, and that is why the sacred messages are deciphered without saying anything. Still, of course, as a deep and powerful tool for personal guidance and advice, during a consultation with the cowrie shell divination, you can ask any questions you want about any subject and area of your life, as Eshu is the force that reveals the mysteries of the universe.

IKIN, OPELÊ IFÁ, AND THE OMO ODUS

Although divinatory consultations with cowrie shells have been used for many decades in Africa and can be found throughout Africa, the cowrie shell divination process that is practiced in Brazil is an adaptation of various rites and traditions brought by enslaved Africans to Brazil since the middle of the eighteenth century. The first Ketu nation emerged between 1788 and 1830 and was called Candomblé Temple. It was founded by three African women, described by Pierre Verger (2002) as "energetic and willing women, originally from Kêto, former freed slaves": Ìyá Adetá, Ìyá Akalá, and Ìyá Nassô, who founded Ilè Àse Ìyá Nasso Oká or, according to Verger, Ìyá Omi Àse Àirá Intilè—also known as Candomblé da Barroquinha, from which the Ketu nation headquarters originated.

> Among the nago, in Bahia, the kétou nation was particularly important, as a result of the numerous wars that, in the early 19th century, opposed the neighboring kingdoms of Abomé and Kétou. It was the latter who created the first Candomblé temples. (Verger 2012)

After being freed from slavery, these three ladies and their descendants made several cultural exchange trips to Africa, bringing back with them knowledge about the religions there. African acquaintances assisted them in organizing, establishing, and maintaining a new black religion in Brazil. José Beniste (2012) points out that, among them, Rodolfo Martins de Andrade (African name Bámbgbósé Obitiko) helped Ìyá Nassô and Obatosi, her successor, in the adaptation of African oracular practices, which until that time were performed only by men. They reorganized the order of Odus to what we know today (Okaran to Alafia), thus allowing them to be used by women, as in Africa the use of Orisha oracles were restricted to men. It is important to note that this reorganization was necessary because, in Africa, religious leaders and access to oracles were, and still are today, exclusively for male use, through the babalawos initiated in the cult of Orunmila. In Brazil during the slave era, it was women who assumed the religious leadership at that time, and therefore, it was necessary to adapt practices to the new reality so that the cult of the Orishas could continue to exist.

Just as the ordination of the Odus was revised, so was the way of interpreting and combining them. In the new method of consulting the cowrie shell divination, the Odu's interpretation is made from several throws of the cowries, each representing one of the sixteen main Odus, and the interconnections among the Odu that presents itself in the consultation moment with the next or the previous one. These adaptations—different from what many authors argue—did not make the cowrie shell divination a less complex or less complete system than traditional African methods like Ikin or Opelê Ifá. On the contrary, even though the number of Odus observed and the ways of identifying them during the consultation decreased (256 in Opele and 16 in Merindilogun), this method created several new ways of composing their combinations—either through secondary moves from the shells that landed closed or through the sequence of five moves to start the consultation.

In the cult of Orunmila, however, the divination of the Odus is done in a totally different way, with two distinct oracles: the Ikin and the Opelê Ifá. In them, the priest interprets each of the 256 possible variations and their myths individually, reciting the numerous corresponding verses to the querent, who then identifies him- or herself with them, and from there, those myths are interpreted.

Both types of consultation are extremely thorough and involve pre- and postconsultation rituals. After identifying the Odu who answers the question, the priest traces with his finger its representative symbol on a ritual table covered with a vegetable powder called *iyerosun*. Each time one of these figures is drawn, the priest says specific prayers and songs to praise the Odu and its Orishas or appease the Odu's negativity. Martins (2013) explains that due to its spiritual importance, complexity, and precision, the Ikin "is used exclusively in ceremonies of greater relevance," whereas consultation through the Opelê Ifá, although it follows the same ritual as the previous one, is a faster process and is therefore used in minor consultations for day-to-day concerns and events.

Taking advantage of the fact that we are talking about spiritual traditions of African origin and the ways in which they have been reconfigured both in Brazil and in Africa, we are going to clarify an important question about the birth Odus and initiations to the Orishas.

Birth Odus and Initiation Odus

In all initiatic traditions in the world, regardless of their origin or the deities they worship, one thing is certain: the main symbolism of initiation rituals is intended to enable you to be reborn, to cease being who you were until then, and to become a new person who, from then on, will be part of this new spiritual group.

In Candomblé and the traditional cult of Ifá, this symbolism gains even more meaning. In their initiation rites, it is necessary to isolate oneself from the outer world for several consecutive days in a room called *honcó*. More than anything else, this room represents the sacred womb, and once inside it, the initiate symbolically dies to the profane world and is reborn among the deities. During this period, the initiate incubates in the room, like a fetus in the womb, little by little becoming a baby, the initiate's new self. Among numerous sacralization rituals, one of them, in particular, is the ritual in which the initiate's personal Odu is identified. At the end of the day, during the public initiation ceremony, the initiate receives a new name, by which he or she will be known from then on among members of this spiritual community.

However, even though many priests insist that the birth Odus can only be identified through these rituals, it is necessary to note *which* birth we are talking about: the biological or the symbolic one. If religious initiation is a symbolic rebirth to the deities, it's natural that from then on there will be a new destiny, so it's also natural that a new Odu is needed for the inititate. This Odu, however, which is commonly called the birth Odu, would be more appropriately called the initiation Odu, because it determines the regency that will guide the inititate, starting from the initiation and going throughout life. On the other hand, there's only one real birth, the biological one, which has no spiritual ties to any belief, divinity, or tradition—even though we're all born from, and as, energies. It is this regency, properly called birth Odus, that we'll deal with and learn about in this book.

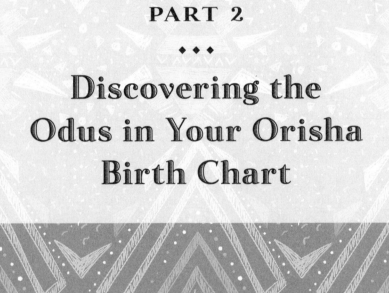

PART 2

• • •

Discovering the Odus in Your Orisha Birth Chart

6

Birth Odus

The Basis of African Numerology

So far, you've learned that the Odus are the roads of destiny, how they act as a means of communication between us and the Orishas, and what the sixteen main Odus are and their meaning in interpretation during consultations with the cowrie shell divination, the Ikin, and the Opelê Ifá oracles. Now the time has come for us to set aside traditional African fundamentals and start learning how these energies and their meanings relate to the construction of our identity and personality through numerology.

Did you know that, from the day you're born, the Odus are related to all areas of your life—such as love, career, and destiny challenges—and govern your choices and the way you live? I'll explain.

In addition to bringing messages from the Orishas about everyday events and guidance on how to solve the problems that happen in your daily life—presenting a picture of how the outer world and its energies influence you in your present moment—the Odus are also related to the moment of your birth and determine important characteristics of your personality: the way you think and feel and the way you relate to other people and the universe. These Odus are called birth Odus and are identified from our date of birth, forming an initial set of six different energies, like an Orisha birth chart or horoscope. Each of these energies corresponds to an area of life, which we also call the major houses of the birth chart: personality, self-identity, career and intellectual evolution, interpersonal and loving relationships, destiny challenges, and inner revolution. Each birth Odu influences our choices and decisions about the specific area of life that it governs, and the main one, called Odu Ori, operates much like the sun sign in an astrological horoscope.

At the same time, in addition to the specific energies of these Odus, which influence various areas of life, each Odu also relates to its specific Orishas, which we learned about in the previous chapter, and is influenced by these Orishas on the specific aspects of the regency being analyzed; numerous and varied relationships form among these Odus and Orishas. Thus, two people with the same regent Odu in one of the houses on the map will be influenced differently by the joint expression of the Odu and the Orishas who manifest themselves in it.

What if there was a way to unravel your own soul and discover the innermost secrets of your personality?

That's exactly what the interpretation of your birth Odus does! A birth chart takes you on a deep dive into yourself. A detailed interpretation of your birth Odus enables you to know and understand your way of loving and relating, of expressing yourself with people, of dealing with your emotions, and of coping with the challenges of the outer world.

From these interpretations and with the conscious work on the positive and negative characteristics they carry, you become able to know yourself better and understand the dynamics that the spiritual world has in your choices and decisions, starting to take them in a more integral and intelligent way. By looking inside yourself and discovering your inner world, you can also count on the strength of the Orishas to help you in your quest for success and happiness, guiding you on your journey of self-knowledge and personal discovery and enabling you to achieve your goals.

As in traditional astrology and numerology, several interpretations and crossovers between these energies can be identified, from the simplest (such as the individual reading of the main Odu of your regency) to the most complex (such as the subcombinations among the six major houses of the Orisha birth chart). The deeper the look, the more detailed information you'll have regarding the personality of each person and the way that person relates to the environment and to him- or herself. Have you ever wanted to understand better how you are influenced by your environment, the people in your life, and your family history and how you in turn exert your influence?

In the next chapters I will teach you in detail how to calculate these birth Odus and interpret them over the six major houses on the map and the four major subcombinations, called minor houses. In an even more detailed analysis, in addition to the six major houses and the four minor houses, it is also possible to identify the influence of the regent Odus of the hour and minute of one's birth, as well as the relationship among all these to the energies that govern their place of birth or the city where you live, the birth Odus of your parents and family, among other combinations.

Talking about these other combinations and assessment possibilities would require a whole new book just to understand their ways of identification and interpretation. So, for now let's leave them aside and focus on the initial study of the ten *major and minor houses.* At the end of the book, after learning what we have ahead of us, I'm going to talk a little bit more about how you can go deeper into these advanced studies—don't worry!

DIFFERENCES BETWEEN COWRIE SHELL DIVINATION AND THE ORISHA BIRTH CHART

Our life and our destiny are the result of two great groups of energies that combine and complement each other: the outer world and the inner world. To start learning about African numerology and the birth Odus, the first lesson and perhaps the most important is understanding this: the big mistake that most people who come to me for advice or consult the cowrie shell divination make is to ignore the balance and interaction of these two energies and only look at one side or the other of this coin, often focusing on just the outer world.

The brighter side of this is that a few people do look intensely into themselves to understand how they deal with their own feelings and emotions. They look at past lessons to avoid repeating them, take real responsibility for their actions, and change some present decisions based on what they find within themselves. Thus, they gradually start to model the results they intend to obtain soon from these changes. The problem is that they usually end up extrapolating some expectations and often confusing responsibility with guilt; they become frustrated for not achieving a certain goal quickly enough or in the way they wanted to and start to punish themselves unconsciously for these apparent shortcomings.

The other side, instead (and which unfortunately is what most people do), happens precisely when they don't look inside themselves or, worse, look and believe that there is nothing to change or improve! They are so used to feeling persecuted by anything and everything in the world, these people constantly have their index finger pointed out: *Jack Doe doesn't like me, so I didn't get that job. John Doe is jealous of me, that's why he convinces everyone that I'm bad. I only did this because Jane Doe did that.* They forget, however, that when one finger points out, three others point in, showing that no matter what happens to us, we'll always have some share of participation and responsibility.

Stop for a moment and answer yourself honestly:
How many people do you know who act like this?
How many times have you told these same lies to yourself?

Of course, there are bad and envious people in the world! Of course, many situations in life are beyond our direct control, and we end up subject to circumstances! The key point in any of these situations is to understand that no matter how intense and conscious our inner work is, no person is an island. We live in a world of energies, and just as we are influenced by them and by our interactions with the people around us, we also influence everything that happens to us and who approaches us.

The truth is that absolutely all situations we live in day to day are the result of these interactions, the sum between the choices we make and other people's choices, whether these choices are positive or negative. Think of this as an invisible scale: on one side we find our personal choices and energies and on the other side are the influences of the world. To achieve the much-desired balance that will guide us to success and happiness, we need to balance both sides. There is a difference between consulting the cowrie shell divination and listening to the voices of the Orishas (the outer world) and understanding the influences of your birth Odus in life (the inner world): one completes, complements, and balances the other, *bringing the outside and inside worlds together.*

Your Orisha birth chart is unique and does not change over time, representing the energies that make up your inner world and how you relate and influence the environment around you. However, this environment changes at every moment, and therefore, the consultation of the cowrie shell divination changes, too! By joining the interpretations of the birth chart and the cowrie shell divination, we become able to understand how the present moment (the outer world) is influencing your path and how your personal energies (the inner world) are influencing your surrounding situation.

It is important to always remember that even if your birth Odus are the same for life, how you will read and interpret their basic characteristics and, especially, how these characteristics will influence you in specific situations of the day to day are changing. Therefore, it is essential that from time to time you reread your Orisha birth chart and try to understand which positive and negative aspects of each Odu are being worked on or ignored in your life!

The first time I made my own Orisha birth chart was amazing: it felt like in a few words my whole life was being described, step by step. But I need to tell you something: it was only when I started looking back at my birth Odus every six months or so that I was able to really understand the influence that every aspect of my personality had over the way I act (and react) in relation to what was happening to me and realized how much I was changing—sometimes for the worse, of course, but most of the time for the better!

I'll give you a real example and briefly tell you about the past twenty years of my life. I started my professional career at age sixteen, and until about age twenty-three or twenty-four, I worked in technology, developing computer software and internet systems. At twenty-four, I made my first major career transition, leaving computers to fully dedicate myself to the Orishas. For the next four or five years, I served hundreds of people through cowrie shell divinations. When I was twenty-nine, I wrote my first book, called *Desvendando Exu,** and from there I started to divide myself among the services in the Orishas temple, a new career as a writer, and eventually my job as editor in chief at Arole Cultural.

Looking at this short time line and how different the activities I've done might seem one to another, can you see how Odu Iorossun defined each one of them? In the beginning, to create computer software, I needed to learn to read and write programming languages, the languages that computers speak. Afterward, as a Babalosha in service to the temple, I needed to understand the messages of the Orishas throughout the cowrie shells and translate them in the best possible way so that people could understand the messages, improving the way I communicated. Now, as an editor and writer, I need more than ever to speak and write clearly and at the same time engagingly, so that you can read with pleasure and learn every lesson I want to convey through my books.

Has my birth Odu changed in all these years? Of course not! But the situations around me, the challenges I experienced, and the opportunities that arose from them changed at every moment. And at each one of them, when I felt in need of answers or guidance, I looked for someone to consult the cowrie shell divination for me and, with its advice, tried to understand how the Orishas' voices could become even

---

*Published in English as *Traditional Brazilian Black Magic* (Rochester, Vt: Destiny Books, 2021).

more positive if I combined them with the potentials that my birth Odus defined in my personality, in my way of being!

So, the real deal is: if you really want to transform your life and awaken your best self through your birth Odus, you need to understand that the main change starts from within. That's why most people keep repeating the same struggles over and over again, always looking for an external solution to inner life's problems: they want everything to change—except themselves! They want their whole life to change, as long as they don't have to leave the comfort zone they've placed themselves in.

By realizing how the major and minor houses on your map interact with each specific situation around you, new personal transformations will happen at every moment, allowing you to grow and evolve toward the desired balance. And when that happens, trust me, you will certainly be many steps along on this journey that we are about to begin!

ELEDA MI: OUR PERSONAL ORISHAS

One of the main concepts of life in society is the principle of identification and belonging: in childhood, we are part of a family, are taken care of by our parents, and attend school, where we seek the care and attention of that special teacher; in adolescence, we expand our circle of friends and begin to explore romantic relationships; and in maturity, we find someone to love and start a family of our own. We all like to feel protected, to be part of a group, to recognize ourselves in the people around us and to feel that they also recognize themselves in us.

In spirituality it happens the same way. Whatever the religion, all have a common belief that each one of us is a divine particle, a little piece of the gods living on Earth. In African-based religions, this sense of affiliation and belonging is intimately linked to what we usually call our *personal Orishas,* also known as the *sacred father or mother,* becoming a complex concept that can be resumed as *spiritual ancestry:* "I am today the result of all those who came before me."

As it happens in physical life since childhood, when our identity and personality are formed by a combination of influences from parents and the family in which we're born, from the people with whom we live, from our personal interpretation of these people and events, in spiritual life this formation also takes place through the combination of a series of energies, especially through the influences of birth Odus and spiritual ancestry. Therefore, we are considered *children* of the Orishas. Thus, the most common question that most people ask when talking about Odus and cowrie shell divination is: *Who are my personal Orishas?* After all, who doesn't want to know who their parents are?

However, it is important that the lessons from the previous chapters have been clear to you so far, as they will be necessary to understand what I am going to say now (even though many authors and priests say otherwise, I take the risk, as those who say otherwise actually don't know the basics of spirituality laws): *neither birth Odus nor any other technique except for the cowrie shell divination or the Opelê Ifá oracle can determine who your personal Orishas are!*

As in physical life, our identity and personality are built from the influences we receive from different people and situations, along with but not restricted to our parents, and as birth Odus are the rulers of how this same identity and personality are defined in the spiritual world, how would mother and father be determined by them? Furthermore, accepting that the birth Odus define who your personal Orishas are would be the same as saying that all people in the world born on the same day as you are children of the same parents!

Therefore, it is essential that this gets very clear so, finally, we can move forward in our study: the birth Odus and the Orisha birth chart are powerful tools for self-knowledge and personal development, but only by consulting the cowrie shell divination or the Opelê Ifá, performed by priests and priestesses truly initiated in the mysteries of these traditions, will you be able to know who your personal Orishas are and to which deity you may or may not be initiated—which, by the way, can be a father and a mother, two fathers or two mothers. Plural families also exist in African spirituality!

HOW TO CALCULATE BIRTH ODUS

Each person has six birth Odus, and each one of them corresponds to one of the six major houses that make up the Orisha birth chart. Two of them deserve special mention: Odu Ori and Osogbo Ori. Odu Ori positively influences all six houses on the map, while Osogbo Ori, also known as the negative birth Odu or placenta Odu, negatively influences them.

Imagine the human body: essentially, we are made up of a head, two arms, two legs, and a heart. For an optimally functioning body, all four appendages plus the head and heart are needed. If by chance we lost an arm or a leg, we could still continue to live; however, if our brain or heart stops, then life ends! Odu Ori and Osogbo Ori function symbolically in the birth chart like the head and the heart and affect the interpretation of all major and minor houses on the map. Each house has its specific regent Odus, but all of the houses are equally influenced by these two main Odus.

To further understand the meaning of the major houses, imagine the human body standing, seen from the front as in figure 3. At the top or crown of the head is Odu Ori, the spiritual head, the connection between matter and spirit. In interpreting the diagram of the Orisha birth chart, Ori is the first and main Odu of birth and somewhat corresponds to the sun sign in astrology. Note that the crown position as a conduit to the spiritual is not unique to African-based religions; other spiritual traditions also see the top of the head as a sacred channel of communication between men and gods—for example, the crown chakra in Hinduism and Tantric Buddhism.

To create a map or diagram, look at da Vinci's drawing and draw an imaginary line from head to toe and another side to side across the chest, forming a cross. In the eye region (number 2 on the drawing) is the second Odu of birth to be calculated, Oju Ori, which symbolically means *what you see or where you look*. At the feet is the third birth Odu (number 3), Ikoko Ori, which symbolically refers to *the steps you take or the way you walk through life*. On the left side of the body, where the

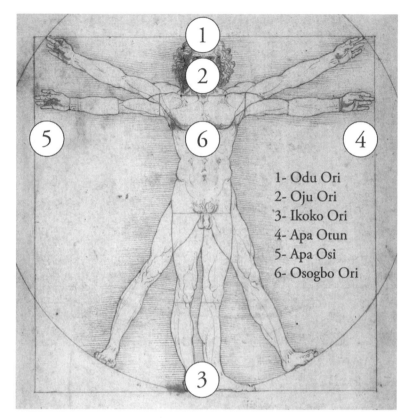

1- Odu Ori
2- Oju Ori
3- Ikoko Ori
4- Apa Otun
5- Apa Osi
6- Osogbo Ori

Fig. 3. The position of the six birth Odus on *The Vitruvian Man*
by Leonardo da Vinci (1490)

heart is located (on the right side of the drawing) is the fourth birth
Odu, Apá Òtún; opposite, on the right side of the body, is the fifth
birth Odu, Apá Osi; and at the intersection of the vertical and horizon-
tal lines is the heart and the sixth Odu of birth, Osogbo Ori, representing *what is inside, hidden, to be transformed*. As noted earlier, Osogbo
Ori is the negative birth Odu.

"Following this logic, does the Odu on the left, in the heart, govern feelings?" you may be asking yourself. Well, sorry to say, the answer
is *no!* Although the heart is commonly the symbol of love, emotions,
and feelings, it is necessary to remember that our connection with
the sacred comes from Ori, the spiritual head, or rather the brain.
Science has determined that the brain is divided into two sides, called

hemispheres, which have different functions: the left hemisphere of the brain is responsible for the functions of logic and theoretical, analytical, and mathematical reasoning, while the right hemisphere is concerned with processing emotions, feelings, and the subjective aspects of our existence. Therefore, the fourth birth Odu, Apá Òtún, is related to the left hemisphere of the brain and governs the rational aspects of our personality, while the fifth birth Odu, Apá Osi, is related to the right hemisphere of the brain, governing the emotional, sentimental, and subjective aspects of life.

To create the Orisha birth chart diagram (figure 4), we will use the same structure as in figure 3: two straight lines perpendicular to each other, forming a cross, noting that house one, which corresponds to Odu Ori, is outside and above the cross. The birth Odus calculations will be performed in the same sequence, from 1 to 6, as explained next. It is important to note that each house is occupied by a single Odu, without combinations and according to the number that represents it, identified by the number of open shells learned earlier.

Therefore, whenever one of the indicated sums is *greater than 16,* we will reduce this number by adding the single digits of the obtained

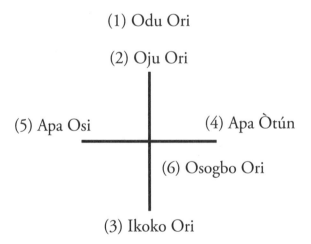

Fig. 4. The diagram for creating the Orisha birth chart

result. For example, if the initial sum results in 36, we will add 3 + 6, reaching 9, which therefore corresponds to Odu Ossa. If, however, the sum is less than or equal to 16, the original is kept.

Calculating Odus for a Birth Date of 09/22/1958

To make it easier to understand how to calculate the birth Odus for the six major houses, we will calculate, as an example, the birth Odus of a person born on September 22, 1958.

Calculating Odu Ori

The calculation to obtain the Odu of house one, Odu Ori, is the only one independent of all the others and is obtained by adding each digit of the person's date of birth. In the example, the result is nine, and therefore the corresponding Odu is Ossa. September is the ninth month, so the addition is as follows:

$$2 + 2 + 0 + 9 + 1 + 9 + 5 + 8 = \mathbf{36} = 3 + 6 = \mathbf{9}$$

Calculating Oju Ori and Ikoko Ori

The second and third Odu of birth, Oju Ori and Ikoko Ori, are obtained by distributing the date of birth digits in pairs over two columns, as follows:

2	2
0	9
1	9
5	8
8	**28**

The result obtained by the sum on the left column represents house two on the map, or Oju Ori; in the example above, the number **8** symbolizes Odu Ejiogbe. The result obtained by summing the digits on the right column represents house three on the map, or Ikoko Ori. In the example, 28 needs to be reduced: 2 + 8 = **10**, which symbolizes Odu Ofun. With these first two results, we can see in figure 5 the partial diagram of an Orisha birth chart for this birth date.

It is from this first composition of the diagram, with the Odus of houses two and three defined, that we will find the corresponding Odus for the next three major houses on the map.

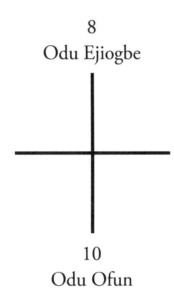

8
Odu Ejiogbe

10
Odu Ofun

Fig. 5. The partial diagram with Odu Ori and Ikoko Ori

Calculating Apá Òtún, Apá Osi, and Osogbo Ori

The Odu corresponding to house four of the map is obtained by the sum of the two previous Odus, 8 and 10, which then must undergo the necessary reduction.

$$8 + 10 = \mathbf{18} = 1 + 8 = \mathbf{9}$$

With this result, house four, or Apá Òtún, therefore, corresponds to Odu Ossa, which is represented by nine opened shells in a cowrie shell divination. The Odu corresponding to house five of the map—

Apá Osi—will then be calculated by the sum of those three previous Odus. See the example:

$$8 + 10 + 9 = \mathbf{27} = 2 + 7 = \mathbf{9}$$

The Apá Osi position, in this case, will also correspond to the Odu Ossa. Finally, house six of the map will be calculated by the sum of all the previous Odus, already duly reduced:

$$8 + 10 + 9 + 9 = \mathbf{36} = 3 + 6 = \mathbf{9}$$

See figure 6 for the final assembly of the diagram for the Orisha birth chart with the example we used so far, based on a birth date of September 22, 1958. Look carefully at the results of the calculated Odus. No, you are not mistaken: houses four, five, and six, as well as the main Odu, Odu Ori, add up to the same result: 9, Odu Ossa.

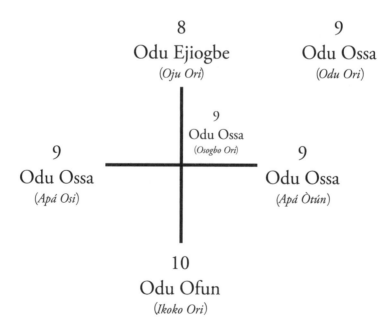

Fig. 6. The complete diagram for a birth date of September 22, 1958

Calculating Odus for a Birth Date of 08/28/1962

The September date illustrates how the same Odu can occupy more than one position on the map. Ossa, however, is special in that it is the only one of all sixteen Odus that can appear in three or more positions—in some cases, it can even occupy all six major houses. Here's another example, illustrating this, for a woman born on August 28, 1962:

1. Odu Ori: $2 + 8 + 0 + 8 + 1 + 9 + 6 + 2 = \mathbf{36} = 3 + 6 = \mathbf{9}$
2. Oju Ori: $2 + 0 + 1 + 6 = \mathbf{9}$
3. Ikoko Ori: $8 + 8 + 9 + 2 = \mathbf{27} = 2 + 7 = \mathbf{9}$
4. Apá Òtún: $9 + 9 = \mathbf{18} = 1 + 8 = \mathbf{9}$
5. Apá Osi: $9 + 9 + 9 = \mathbf{27} = 2 + 7 = \mathbf{9}$
6. Osogbo Ori: $9 + 9 + 9 + 9 = \mathbf{36} = 3 + 6 = \mathbf{9}$

So, when Odu Ossa occupies all houses, does it mean that this Odu will be interpreted in the same way? Absolutely not! Even though we have the same Odu in all positions, it is necessary to remember that a correct interpretation of the Odu's influence must consider its ruling context, along with the gender of the person for whom the map is interpreted, combined with the vibrational gender of each Odu, observing how this energy adapts through it.

In our previous example, we have the Odu Ossa conducting Apá Òtún, career, and Apá Osi, relationships. As Ossa is the Odu of independence and freedom, in Apá Òtún it will mainly indicate that the person has means for owning a business or working as an independent consultant. Odu Ossa is also the path of passion and female sexual activity; therefore, in Apá Osi, it will indicate intense relationships, including some bordering on jealousy and possessiveness.

Another curiosity, which we will understand better when learning about the interpretation of each Odu for house one, is that just as Ossa is the only Odu that can occupy all six houses simultaneously, Odu Okaran will never occupy any house—after all, no sum can result in 1. Before we begin to learn the meanings of each major house, let's take a look at one more example in detail, this time in which none of the Odus repeats itself: April 26, 1993.

Calculating Odu Ori

Adding the birth digits individually:

$$2 + 6 + 0 + 4 + 1 + 9 + 9 + 3 = \mathbf{34} = 3 + 4 = \mathbf{7}$$

Odu Ori = 7 = Odu Odi

Calculating Oju Ori and Ikoko Ori

By distributing the date of birth digit pairs in two columns and reducing the results greater than 16:

$$
\begin{array}{c|c}
2 & 6 \\
0 & 4 \\
1 & 9 \\
9 & 3 \\
\hline
\mathbf{12} & \mathbf{22}
\end{array}
$$

Oju Ori = 12 = Odu Ejilaxebora
Ikoko Ori = 22 = 2 + 2 = **4 = Odu Iorossun**

Calculating Apá Òtún, Apá Osi, and Osogbo Ori

From the result obtained in the previous calculation, already reduced and positioned in the diagram, sum the results of each previous house sequentially, with the appropriate reductions:

Apá Òtún = 12 + 4 = **16 = Odu Alafia**
Apá Osi = 12 + 4 + 16 = 32 = 3 + 2 = **5 = Odu Oshe**
Osogbo Ori = 12 + 4 + 16 + 5 = 37 = 3 + 7 = **10 = Odu Ofun**

Note that the sequence of calculations must follow the order indicated, as their results always depend on the previous result.

Map Assembly Result

Placing the birth Odus in the corresponding houses, note that the Odus are all different from one another:

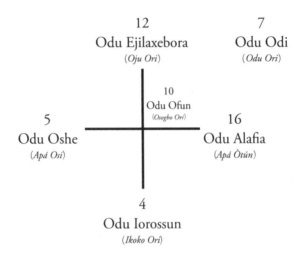

Fig. 7. The complete diagram for someone born on April 26, 1993.

◖ Calculating Your Own Birth Odus

Now, let's do a quick exercise and calculate your own birth Odus without trying to interpret them yet.

1. My date of birth is _____ / _____ / _____ .
2. Adding all the digits of the complete date, I will find the Odu corresponding to house one of my Orisha birth chart:

_____ + _____ + _____ + _____ + _____ + _____ + _____ + _____ = _____
day   day   month   month   year   year   year   year

If it is greater than 16, make the reduction: _____ + _____ = _____
My birth Odu is _____ .

3. Now, distributing the pairs of digits into two columns to calculate Odu Ori and Ikoko Ori:

_____D_____ | _____D_____
_____M_____ | _____M_____
_____Y_____ | _____Y_____
_____Y_____ | _____Y_____

The sum already reduced in the left column is _____, so the Odu that corresponds to my Oju Ori is _____.

The sum already reduced in the column on the right is _____, and hence the Odu that corresponds to my Ikoko Ori is _____.

4. Adding the result of Odu Ori + Ikoko Ori, I will find the sum that corresponds to house four: _____ + _____ = _____

If it is greater than 16, make the reduction: _____ + _____ = _____
With that, my Odu in Apá Òtún is _____.

5. Adding the result of Odu Ori + Ikoko Ori + Apá Òtún, I will find the sum that corresponds to house five, always remembering to reduce until the result is less than or equal to 16:

_____ + _____ + _____ = _____ = _____ + _____ = _____
With that, my Odu in Apá Osi is _____.

6. Again, adding all the previous results already reduced, I will find the sum that corresponds to house six, the negative Odu of my birth:

_____ + _____ + _____ + _____ = _____

If it is greater than 16, make the reduction : _____ + _____ = _____
With that, my Odu in Osogbo Ori is _____.

THE SIX MAJOR HOUSES
OF THE
ORISHA BIRTH CHART

As we could see in the previous examples, as well as in the descriptions of each of the sixteen main Odus, each position of the birth Odus in the Orisha birth chart needs to be interpreted considering some fundamental aspects:

- The area of life that the house rules
- The characteristics and energies of the resulting Odu
- The characteristics of the Orishas related to this Odu

- The gender of the person whose map is being done, noting the *gender identity* and not the *biological sex*
- The Odus in Odu Ori and Osogbo Ori positions

The following descriptions outline the aspects that can be inferred from the interpretation of each of the six major houses in relation to the area of life to which each relates. For a correct interpretation of the Orisha birth chart, the characteristics and energies of each Odu, as earlier, must be contextualized in regard to these aspects, considering the other items presented in the list, such as gender, Odu Ori and Osogbo Ori, and the Orisha of initiation of the person (if any), along with individual aspects that you identify while making the map, according to each case.

Odu Ori: Identity and Personality

The first and main house of the Orisha birth chart receives the main Odu of birth, which can be identified through African numerology and positively influences all others. Odu Ori defines who you truly are and, at the same time, the way you present yourself and express yourself in life and how you are recognized by the outer world, indicating how and in what way you find happiness and meaning in your life.

Who am I really?
And who do I prove to be?

By understanding the ways in which this energy defines your identity and personality, you can neutralize the negative nuances about how the outer world perceives you and enhance the ways in which you are seen by the environment around you, becoming more endearing and charismatic.

Oju Ori: Temperament and Intellect

In the second house of the map is the Odu that defines how you see and interpret the reality around you, your most intimate desires, your values and ideals. It is this Odu that indicates how you internalize what comes to you from the outside, how you absorb external influences, how you react to them, and how you transform them before receiving them into you.

Oju Ori also determines the reach of your personal horizon, your ability to find opportunities inside yourself and in the environment around you to set life goals—or to escape reality through fantasy rather than recognize the truth in front of you.

How do I perceive the world around me?
How big do I see myself?
How do I set my priorities?

As you understand the influences of the regent Odu of this house and meditate on real-life issues, as well as the way you set your goals in contrast with how you perceive yourself versus the way the world sees you, you become capable of setting your goals in a more creative and conscious way, equalizing your achievements and minimizing frustrations.

Ikoko Ori: Personal Evolution

The third major house of the Orisha birth chart is the Odu that defines the way you walk your path from where you are right now until you attain your most desired goals and the means with which you strive to achieve what you want. In addition, this is also the Odu that provides advice regarding the challenges you'll have to face during your life's journey and the benefits that you'll be able to obtain and enjoy as you meet each challenge.

Where do I want to and where do I allow myself to go?
What strategies do I implement to do so?
How do I advance and evolve over and despite difficulties?

Realizing how the Odus influence the way you progress in the face of destiny challenges, walk through life to achieve your goals, and struggle to get what you want, it is possible to prepare yourself to minimize the difficulties and negative influences and face them with a lighter heart, anticipating the positive opportunities that will arise during the journey and allowing yourself to better enjoy each step and result.

Apá Òtún: Material World, Career, and Finance

In Apá Òtún, the fourth major house in an Orisha birth chart, is the Odu that defines your practical and objective reality, material issues, rational aspects of your life, and how you use your intellectual abilities and reasoning. For this reason, it is also this Odu that provides guidance concerning which fields of study and professional activity are favorable to you, as well as the best ways to develop you career and improve your finances.

What do I consider prosperity?

What is my relationship with money and wealth?

Do I develop and apply my intellectual potentials to achieve my material goals?

In many cases we will find the same regent Odu in both Odu Ori and Apá Òtún, indicating that the ways you see yourself and how you are seen by the world directly interfere with the ways you apply the potentials of the outer world in your daily life. Furthermore, Apá Òtún and Apá Osi act on broad aspects of your personality, basically dividing them into rational/material and emotional/sentimental. For this reason, to carry out an in-depth assessment of how these birth Odus define each specific point of who you are and how you live, it is also necessary to establish the Odus on the minor houses of your map, which will address these specific nuances, as we will see later.

Apá Osi: Relationships and Sexuality

No person in the world can live without relating to others. Be it family, romantic, professional, or social relationships, we are all subject to the encounters and mismatches of fate, and in each encounter, new relationships and interactions are formed and new energies are combined or conflicted. The regency of the fifth major house on the map acts on these dynamics: Apá Osi is the Odu that governs your emotions and feelings, psychological traumas, self-esteem, and the ways in which you relate to people around you.

Am I able to give and receive affection?
Do I treat people around me as I would like to be treated?
Do I accept and work on my bad feelings, or do I delude
myself with the utopia of goodness?

Through the interpretation of this Odu, it is possible to understand the most subjective aspects of your life—your way of giving and receiving affection, of loving and being loved. Thus, its influences, negativities, and potentials allow you to develop greater understanding, compassion, and empathy between you and the people with whom you relate.

Osogbo Ori: Challenges and Inner Revolution

As noted earlier, the sixth major house of the Orisha birth chart, Osogbo Ori, is also called the placenta Odu or negative birth Odu. As paradoxical as it may seem, it does not act directly on any area of life but instead interferes in all other major and minor houses and in all other Odus that might be influencing us—whether they are the birth Odus of the inner world or the Odus identified through consultations of the cowrie shell divination of the outer world—and negating their actions in our lives. Precisely for this reason, alongside Odu Ori, this is the most important map house: it is this birth Odu that determines which personal challenges to overcome and the lessons we must learn through pain or love throughout our existence.

Looking at the problems of the past, what similarities do I see in
comparison to the problems of the present?
What are the biggest negative characteristics I see in myself,
and how can I change them?

Though it may seem perverse and cruel, only through a deep and detailed analysis of the energies of this Odu—the way it affects our other birth Odus and especially how it has influenced past experiences—will we be able to truly understand what direction to carry out our inner revolution and be reborn in life. Once this dynamic is understood and we make it our mission to recognize all the situations that happen in our lives that are directly linked to the choices we make, we will finally understand that our choices are obviously influenced by the negative aspects of our personality. When you realize that you can consciously act to neutralize this Odu's influence, you will become capable of transforming everyday difficulties into opportunities for personal evolution. From there, you will be able to overcome the negative characteristics of your personality and break your harmful repetitive cycles and learn to accept the human condition.

THE FOUR MINOR HOUSES OF THE ORISHA BIRTH CHART

The four minor houses of the Orisha birth chart are directly related to the combination of the two major house as quadrants of the map, and we must contextualize their meanings so that we can effectively understand them. Interpreting the four minor houses involves hard work and dedication to look inside and honestly recognize your way of being and thinking about yourself, admit your flaws, and realize which ones you can work on now, as well as recognizing the positive aspects of each one of them.

*Only by facing your shadow and recognizing yourself
in it will you be able to illuminate it.*

Through the analysis of the four minor houses on the map you will unravel the more subtle nuances that are revealed when we consider all aspects of their combinations: Odus, Orishas of the path, psychosocial formation, life experiences, emotional aspects, and so on. It is also in the interpretation of the four minor houses that Plato's Myth of the Cave, which I discuss in detail in chapter 8, makes even more sense, for it is in these interpretations that the work of deep transformation begins.

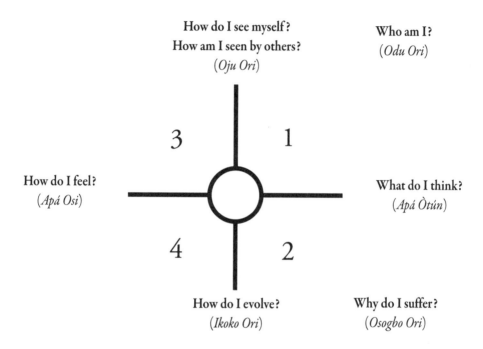

Fig. 8. The basic aspects of each major house.

So that we can better understand these intersections and interpretations, take a minute to meditate over the questions in figure 8. They're just a few possible guides to start understanding the contexts of the minor houses, their meanings, and the ways in which unveiling their nuances can indicate the ways to act on specific issues of personality, both to enhance and to neutralize their influence.

◖ *Creating Your Own Orisha Birth Chart*

Before we go any further, how about starting to create your own Orisha birth chart? With the Odus you calculated in the previous exercise, fill in the following diagram.

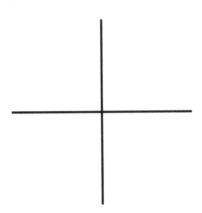

HOW TO CALCULATE MINOR HOUSES

There are two options for calculating the Odus of the minor houses: obtaining a single Odu for each quadrant, which is the simplified way to do it, or obtaining two Odus per quadrant, identifying both a positive and a negative aspect of the house in question, thereby engaging in a deeper analysis. Both ways are obtained by adding the major house equivalent number of a given quadrant.

To ease understanding, let's take as an example the birth chart already created for the date April 26, 1993. The calculation of the minor house Odus on the map follows the same rule as before: from 2 to 16, reducing the results when necessary. Figure 9 shows the results for the example. You will see that quadrants one and two complete each other, as do quadrants three and four:

> Quadrant one: Oju Ori + Apá Òtún
> 12 + 16 = 28 = 2 + 8 = 10 = Odu Ofun
> Quadrant two: Apá Òtún + Ikoko Ori
> 16 + 4 = 20 = 2 + 0 = 2 = Odu Ejioko

Quadrant three: Oju Ori + Apá Osi

12 + 5 = 17 = 1 + 7 = 8 = Odu Ejiogbe

Quadrant four: Apá Osi + Ikoko Ori

5 + 4 = 9 = Odu Ossa

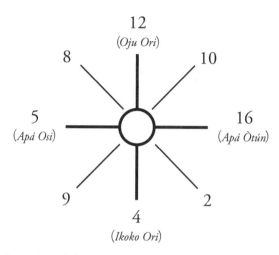

Fig. 9. The Odus of the major and minor houses for a birth date
of April 26, 1993

Also, you must remember that *Odu Ori positively influences all houses on the map,* just as *Osogbo Ori influences them negatively.* In this way, if we want to advance in the interpretation of the minor houses, we can split them in these two aspects, including the positive or negative Odu in the calculation and thus obtaining two regent Odus for each minor house:

Quadrant One
Positive: Oju Ori + Apá Òtún + Odu Ori
12 + 16 + 7 = 35 = 3 + 5 = **8** = **Odu Ejiogbe**
Negative: Oju Ori + Apá Òtún + Osogbo Ori
12 + 16 + 10 = 38 = 3 + 8 = **11** = **Odu Owarin**

Quadrant Two
Positive: Apá Òtún + Ikoko Ori + Odu Ori
16 + 4 + 7 = 27 = 2 + 7 = **9** = **Odu Ossa**
Negative: Apá Òtún + Ikoko Ori + Osogbo Ori
16 + 4 + 10 = 30 = 3 + 0 = **3** = **Odu Ogunda**
Quadrant Three
Positive: Oju Ori + Apá Osi + Odu Ori
12 + 5 + 7 = 24 = 2 + 4 = **6** = **Odu Obara**
Negative: Oju Ori + Apá Osi + Osogbo Ori
12 + 5 + 10 = 27 = 2 + 7 = **9** = **Odu Ossa**
Quadrant Four
Positive: Apá Osi + Ikoko Ori + Odu Ori
5 + 4 + 7 = **16** = **Odu Alafia**
Negative: Apá Osi + Ikoko Ori + Osogbo Ori
5 + 4 + 10 = 19 = 1 + 9 = **10** = **Odu Ofun**

Having understood the calculations and variations of the minor houses, let us then move on to explaining the meanings of each one of them.

Quadrant One: Oju Ori + Apá Òtún

This combination of the regency defines how you see yourself, the ways in which the outer world perceives you, or, better said, how you show yourself to the outer world and your ability to see horizons, set goals and objectives, and establish priorities and strategies to reach them (Oju Ori) with the regency that determines your intellectual potential, your relationship with money and the material aspects of existence, and your analytical and reasoning capabilities (Apá Òtún). From this minor house, we will understand in more detail your ability to identify new business opportunities and new practical partnerships; your skills for managing personal and professional crises; and your sense of intellectual empathy (the ability to perceive what and how other people think and how they react to reality) in opposition to emotional empathy (the ability to feel in yourself what others feel).

The main point here is to understand how the demands of adult life, your commitments and responsibilities, your financial organization, and your dedication to study and intellectual development (or lack thereof) affect the ways you perceive yourself as an individual and interfere with your self-esteem. Observing the positive aspects of the Odu identified here can point out important characteristics to be developed so that the *image you convey* about who you are in face of the day-to-day demands is closer to the *image you have of yourself* in relation to your productive capacity, your beliefs about financial worthiness, and your personal priorities and goals.

Quadrant one asks: Do I plan the steps needed to get where I want to go? Are my efforts valued by others and myself? Do I work at a profession I like, and does my work give me pleasure? Do I apply my main positive characteristics to building a responsible and committed image?

The negative characteristics of the regent Odu on quadrant one may indicate fundamental aspects that need to be corrected for you to start achieving your personal goals and objectives while demonstrating commitment to the demands of adult life, which will often be beyond our capacity to control. Some examples are procrastinating, sabotaging yourself at work, neglecting your studies at school, or mismanaging your finances.

◖ Let's Calculate Your Quadrant One

The simple way:

_____ (Oju Ori) + _____ (Apá Òtún) = _____

Reducing if necessary: _____ + _____ = _____

Calculating the positive aspect:

_____ (Odu Ori) + _____ (Oju Ori) + _____ (Apá Òtún) = _____

Reducing if necessary: _____ + _____ = _____

Calculating the negative aspect:

_____ (Osogbo Ori) + _____ (Oju Ori) + _____ (Apá Òtún) = _____

Reducing if necessary: _____ + _____ = _____

Quadrant Two: Ikoko Ori + Apá Òtún

This combination of the regency defines the way you make headway or remain stagnant in the face of adversity, how you plan your future and set goals, and how you make decisions and take the necessary steps toward your desires and goals (Ikoko Ori) with the regency that determines your intellectual potential, your relationship with money and the material aspects of existence, and your analytical and reasoning capabilities (Apá Òtún). From this Odu, we will understand in more detail if and how you turn your goals and objectives into reality (whereas the Odu in quadrant one thinks and plans, the Odu in quadrant two makes this planning real); your ability to effectively make decisions and put into practice what you have planned for your professional and material life; how you act and react to situations of stress and pressure at work or school; your leadership and management instincts; and the ways you handle money (which is different from your perception of prosperity and wealth, which is governed by the Odu of quadrant one).

The main reflection here is to see if you truly seek and act to achieve and complete the practical and material goals you have set for your life, or if, even knowing what you want, you resist change, postpone obligations and commitments, and/or abandon your plans when difficulties and challenges present themselves. Observing the positive aspects of the Odu identified in this quadrant can point out fundamental aspects so that the actions and attitudes you take in the present are aligned with what you need now and what you want for your future. In addition, it also indicates the best characteristics to develop so that the relationship between effort undertaken and rewards received in your work or field of study can be multiplied.

Quadrant two asks: Do I do what must be done to get where I want to be? Do I seek to improve myself professionally and intellectually, taking courses and improving my skills, to grow in my career? Am I able to fulfill a schedule of tasks without outside activities taking my focus? And, above all, how do I act today to achieve the goals I set for my tomorrow?

In the same way, noticing the negative characteristics of the regent Odu on quadrant two can indicate the key points that need to be corrected for you to take your plans and desires from the dream world and bring them into reality. These characteristics can show you how to avoid the frustration of not accomplishing your goals or abandoning them and help you understand how we often look at the macro and forget about the micro, making it necessary to set intermediate goals. In that sense, there is a saying that sums it up very well: done is better than perfect!

◐ Let's Calculate Your Quadrant Two

The simple way:

_____ (Oju Ori) + _____ (Apá Òtún) = _____

Reducing if necessary: _____ + _____ = _____

Calculating the positive aspect:

_____ (Odu Ori) + _____ (Oju Ori) + _____ (Apá Òtún) = _____

Reducing if necessary: _____ + _____ = _____

Calculating the negative aspect:

_____ (Osogbo Ori) + _____ (Oju Ori) + _____ (Apá Òtún) = _____

Reducing if necessary: _____ + _____ = _____

Quadrant Three: Oju Ori + Apá Osi

This combination defines how you see yourself, the ways you present yourself to the outer world, your self-esteem and self-confidence, your ability to dream and set goals, your perception of yourself, and how you imagine you are perceived (Oju Ori) with the regency that determines your social interactions, the ways you deal with your feelings, your capacity for emotional empathy (the ability to perceive what the other feels and share this feeling with that person), which is different from intellectual empathy (the ability to perceive what the other thinks and how the other reacts to reality), the ways you give and receive affection, and the ways in which you interact with the people around you—whether they are family, romantic, or social relationships

(Apá Osi). From this Odu it will be possible to perceive the ways in which, positively or negatively, you imprint your personality and temperament on the people around you or, on the contrary, how you are influenced by the personalities of the people with whom you live. It is also from this Odu that you can better identify the nuances of your relationships, your sexual desires and fantasies, and the relationship you have with your own body (whether erotic or how well you accept your physical characteristics).

The main reflection in quadrant three is to understand how you affect the environment around you by imposing your wishes and desires or submitting to those of others; in the same way, it is also necessary to think about how you allow yourself to be influenced by the people around you in relation to your self-esteem and sense of self-worth. One of the most important aspects to note here is the characteristic that we call *behavior* in the interpretation of birth Odus, as we will see in the next chapter. The *behavioral assessment* of the birth Odu in quadrants three and four has a fundamental influence on the relationship you have with your body and with your sexuality.

Quadrant three asks: Do I express my opinions, desires, and wishes to others while respecting theirs? Do I recognize my own worth and my limitations, not allowing others' opinions to interfere with how I perceive myself? Do I understand what my true role is in the lives of the people with whom I live and what their roles are in mine and avoid crossing boundaries or inverting social roles and functions? Do I express my positive and negative feelings in a balanced way, honestly but not aggressively? Can I receive both criticism and praise?

Observing the positive aspects of quadrant three's Odu can help you identify the ways in which you inspire the people around you through the subtle ways you act and interact with them, which you may not have noticed before. It will show you how others feel welcomed and recognized by you and the ways in which you can influence them to act and think by consciously using and shaping the image you have of yourself and the one(s) others have of you. In the romantic and sexual aspect, this Odu can also indicate the ways in which you relate emotionally, the affective bonds that you develop and that you expect from your partner, and the potential for the exchange of affection; it can show you how you stimulate your libido through fantasies and fetishes and how you can improve your relationship with your own body and with the bodies of those you relate to. In the family aspect, it is the Odu on quadrant three that will indicate the social roles you have in the family and how you give and receive within it, the emotional bonds between you and your parents or children, and your ability, even while maintaining these bonds, to live in a unique and independent way.

Observing the negative characteristics of the regent Odu of quadrant three, in turn, can indicate nuances about how you impose your will and desires without recognizing and respecting other people's will, often acting with selfishness and tyranny; on the contrary, it can show you how you allow yourself to be dominated and subjugated. The negative influences of this Odu can also indicate the reversal of father/mother roles, making you assume responsibilities that are not yours (such as assuming the role of parent with your own parents, or the opposite—putting your children in this position). In love relationships, especially, the negative side of this Odu can present sensitive issues such as tendencies to psychological and emotional violence (whether as an aggressor or as a victim), extrapolation of sexual limits, difficulties in creating bonds, self-sabotaging of your relationships, tendencies to fall in love with toxic people as a way of unknowingly punishing yourself, and a lack or excess libido and its attendant frigidity or depravity.

◖ Let's Calculate Your Quadrant Three

The simple way:

_____ (Oju Ori) + _____ (Apá Òtún) = _____

Reducing if necessary: _____ + _____ = _____

Calculating the positive aspect:

_____ (Odu Ori) + _____ (Oju Ori) + _____ (Apá Òtún) = _____

Reducing if necessary: _____ + _____ = _____

Calculating the negative aspect:

_____ (Osogbo Ori) + _____ (Oju Ori) + _____ (Apá Òtún) = _____

Reducing if necessary: _____ + _____ = _____

Quadrant Four: Ikoko Ori + Apá Osi

This combination with the regency defines how you act in practical terms and make what you have dreamed or idealized into a reality, how you develop or suppress your desires (or the desires of others), how you demonstrate and assert your individuality (Ikoko Ori) with the regency that defines your ways of relating to people and the environment, your ways of empathizing with and respecting other people's feelings, your ability to love and allow yourself to be loved, your interactions in social relationships, and your relationships in the broadest sense (Apá Osi). Through the interpretation of this birth Odu, it will be possible to equalize what is desired positively or negatively with what can actually be accomplished (whereas the quadrant three Odu fantasizes and daydreams, the quadrant four Odu puts into practice what was imagined); and to understand the nuances of how you engage in your personal relationships and exchange experiences, knowledge, and pleasure and the ways in which you defend your opinions (or let yourself be dominated and manipulated by the opinions of others), accepting that though the opinions of others may be different from yours this does not hurt your personal truth.

The main reflection here is to identify whether your feelings, emotions, and opinions—whether they are in relation to family, partner, friends, and colleagues—are being expressed correctly and, especially, how you react to the feelings, emotions, and opinions of others. Many problems in relationships happen because we assume others see and understand how we feel without noticing whether we are communicating what we want. In the opposite direction, people around us also act like this, whether out of malice or fear: they expect us to know their expectations and wishes without clearly communicating them. It's a bit like hearing "that's not what I meant" and realizing that the only possible answer is "but that's what you said." Remember that while Odu Ori and the other birth Odus related to it define *what we think and imagine being or doing,* it is Ikoko Ori and the other birth Odus linked to it that define *what we actually do, demonstrate, and perform.*

Therefore, quadrant four asks: Do I accept my physical body as it is without guilt? Do I actively take care of my physical and mental health, seeking to develop healthy habits? Do I respect the sexual and affective desires, fantasies, and limits of the people around me at the same time as I try to fulfill my desires and fantasies in a balanced way? Do I pay attention to each person who passes my way, treating him or her with respect and recognition, regardless of his or her social or financial status? Does my attitude, my tone of voice, and my way of behaving convey aggression or acceptance? Do I know how to recognize and act when a relationship—social, professional, familial, or love—proves to be toxic or harmful and leave it, or do I remain stuck in it even when it hurts me?

The positive aspects of the Odu in this quadrant will help you to understand how you touch the hearts of those around you and how you can thereby become an inspiration through example, generosity, sincere affection, and compassion. In addition, it can also indicate the best characteristics to be developed so that your relationships are balanced and healthy, since it is through the exchange of care that love is built. This starts with you first developing self-love and then recognizing the love that exists in others. Likewise, as the quadrant four Odu is linked both to emotions and sexuality, it will also show potentialities to be developed in your way of feeling pleasure and enjoying your body and sex, alone or with someone else.

On the other hand, observing the negative characteristics of this regent Odu can alert you to physical and emotional imbalances regarding your relationship with your body and the bodies of others, which come out of the imaginary and enter the real world, either by conscious actions or by the somatization of traumas. This Odu also points out how you interact with people, socially and sexually, how you treat them, and how you allow yourself to be treated. It indicates the key points that need to be corrected so that you can learn to exchange feelings and affections (and, with them, energies) and, in more serious and specific cases, to acknowledge and overcome tendencies toward physical and sexual violence.

◐ Let's Calculate Your Quadrant Four

The simple way:

_____ (Oju Ori) + _____ (Apá Òtún) = _____

Reducing if necessary: _____ + _____ = _____

Calculating the positive aspect:

____ (Odu Ori) + ____ (Oju Ori) + ____ (Apá Òtún) = _____

Reducing if necessary: _____ + _____ = _____

Calculating the negative aspect:

____ (Osogbo Ori) + ____ (Oju Ori) + ____ (Apá Òtún) = ____

Reducing if necessary: _____ + _____ = _____

7

The Orisha Birth Chart

The interpretation of the birth Odu, as we have already seen, goes far beyond simply knowing the basic characteristics of the sixteen main Odus. It is necessary to observe the energetic vibration of them, the element of nature to which it relates, the gender of the person for whom the map is set up, and, above all, the meanings and nuances of each major or minor house to which it is interpreted. Based on the assessments of each of these factors and the contexts of each house, we will ultimately form the Orisha birth chart and will be able to carry out a deep analysis of the personality, identity, temperament, and challenges of each person's destiny.

Some important points to clarify, however, are linked to these characteristics and need to be understood very clearly so that the analyses learned in this book are not confused. The first of them is to be sure that descriptions you will learn next are related to birth and personality archetypes related to the sixteen main Odus and have no direct bearing on the interpretations of those same Odus when in an oracular consultation.

Another fundamental aspect to emphasize is that the *energetic vibration* of the Odu has nothing to do with the gender of the Orishas they are related to, much less the biological gender or gender identity of the person for whom the map is interpreted. Here, the definitions of masculine and feminine are related to the traditional definitions of the

Odus in the Ifá corpus—the collection of traditional Orishas myths—and to concepts commonly identified with these energies: masculine refers to the active principle of the universe, to excitement, agitation, and movement and is considered hot or positive; and feminine refers to the passive principle of the universe, to tranquillity, calm, and rest and is considered cold or negative.

The same observation applies to the element of nature (earth, fire, water, air) to which each Odu corresponds. As you'll see in the descriptions ahead, each Odu corresponds to two elements, always with a predominance of the first. In this way, remember the principle of energy balance we discussed earlier: of the sixteen Odus, eight will be male and eight will be female; thus, also, four will have predominance of the earth element, four of the fire element, four of the water element, and four of the air element. Each set of four Odus with a predominance of the fire element, for example, will have as a secondary element, one of the same four mentioned elements and may even be characterized by *fire, fire.*

In addition to these aspects, which are intimately connected with the spiritual and energetic issues of both the Odus and the Orishas that influence them, another essential aspect in the evaluation of the birth Odus concerns what we will call *Odu behavioral style,* relating to the house map or the interpretation that is being made. Before moving on to the interpretations and characteristics of birth Odus in African numerology, let's better understand what they are and how Odu behavioral styles influence our interpretation.

BIRTH ODU BEHAVIORAL STYLES

The behavioral style of a given birth Odu can also be defined as the personality profile of this energy that, like all other characteristics, influences the person ruled by it. Like the elements of nature, the four positive and negative behaviors of the Odus intertwine with one another, and even though each of them has its direct opposite, they can appear in each of the sixteen Odus under all possible combinations.

However, it is important to emphasize that this classification does not concern character in an ethical or moral sense of the person being evaluated. The Odus, as well as those who interpret them, have a duty to abstain from moral judgments when interpreting the map. Unlike Judeo-Christian and most Western religions, the Afro-religious ethos does not recognize the good-evil dichotomy and understands that it isn't the action by itself but the circumstances that lead to the action that have weight and value. Odu behavioral styles indicate, in general terms, the main archetype from which our interpretations will be based, indicating the postures and behaviors adopted by the person when faced with certain stimuli and situations.

According to *Merriam-Webster's Collegiate Dictionary*, among the definitions of the word *behavior* are "the way in which someone conducts oneself or behaves" and "the response of an individual, group, or species to its environment." With these two definitions in mind, the interpretation of the *behavioral* aspect of an Odu becomes clearer. For example, some people work better under pressure, while others work more efficiently when they have flexible deadlines. Some people seem to make friends easily and can chat for hours on end with someone they've just met, while others find it difficult to talk for a long time even with someone they've known for years.

It is also important to realize that an Odu's behavioral style can significantly interfere in a person's behavior throughout life, but analyzing experiences and situations from the past, as well as conscious work on the Odu's positive and negative characteristics, can change the way this influence happens. It is clear, therefore, that all these influences are interconnected, and the interpretation of all of them together is what guarantees a correct and in-depth analysis of birth Odus; even so, the analysis of Odu behavioral styles is the first step toward the interpretation of the Orisha birth chart.

Furthermore, as it happens with the analysis of all other aspects of the Orisha birth chart, although each major and minor house has its own regent Odu, the *positive behavior* of Odu Ori and the *negative behavior* of Osogbo Ori will influence them all. For this reason, it is necessary to understand that the same person can demonstrate characteristics of more than one behavioral style. In fact, this situation is quite common—for example, a person can be extremely methodical and organized (*analytical behavior*) but also have great communication skills with his or her work team (*extroverted behavior*). In this case, the Odu fits into more than one profile; even so, one of them—or rather two: one positive, the other negative—will always be more present in their behavior and should be explored further in the interpretations of map houses and its regent Odus, according to the context of each one of them.

As we become able to identify the most outstanding behavior in ourselves and in the people who live with us, it becomes easier to adapt and model that behavior so that we can transform ourselves and others. At first, this may seem like a difficult task for most people, but with a little patience and practice, this assessment will become natural to the point where you don't have to think about it: your brain will recognize the required combination for this or that moment and will make the necessary skills available.

Next, we will get to know the four positive and negative behaviors and the main definitions of each of them. It is worth remembering, however, that one does not nullify the other and that there is no right or wrong in being ruled by any of them: we are talking about behavioral traits, energies that combine and transform in each situation.

Dominant/Impulsive

Key words: *speed, urgency, agility, daring, leadership, proactivity, competitiveness*

The *dominant behavior person* has three basic needs: to be in control of situations, to be right when arguing, and to be in constant evolution and growth. For this reason, people governed by this behavior have the ability to constantly reinvent themselves, developing new skills and potential precisely to meet their needs to move forward and remain in control: the world changes, and, therefore, the dominants change too.

Do you know the kind of person who, even in silence, always has an air of sobriety and leadership? Who talks and always seems to be giving an order or command, even when he wants to be affectionate? The kind of person who always has an answer or argument at her fingertips to show that their opinion is correct? This is the dominant.

Those ruled by a *dominant behavior Odu* love a challenge and seem to be forever in competition with themselves and the world around them. Their actions, in general, demonstrate courage and affinity with obstacles and difficulties—after all, without obstacles, they would not be able to prove that they can win all the time.

Dominant behavior people are achievers and go to great lengths to do and achieve what they want, becoming extremely versatile when it matters to them: they expand and conquer, at whatever the cost. They are leaders by nature, extremely demanding with themselves and with the people around them, and for this reason they have a keen ability to identify what needs to be done and the best moment to do it. However, because they want things to always be their way, they have immense difficulty in delegating tasks and dividing responsibilities.

The downside of this behavior, which we call *impulsive,* is that because they are always in search of perfection and achievement, they often set goals that are almost unattainable. With that, dominant people end up spending unnecessary time and effort just to be able to say, "I did it." They also have difficulty working in groups and recognizing that someone else's opinion or work may eventually be better than theirs.

Dominants' self-confidence is often confused with arrogance: the dominant/impulsives don't think so; they're sure of everything! Furthermore, people under this behavioral style do not easily give up what they want and have difficulties respecting rules and limits. On the other hand, when in positions of power and leadership, they can easily become dictatorial and authoritarian.

If in the positive aspect dominants are excellent leaders, in their negative aspect they run a great risk of becoming lonely people. Furthermore, in this aspect their attitudes and decisions are made by emotion rather than reason. Their blood boils, and they end up being forced to pay the price of their own choices without reaping the rewards of victory.

Extrovert/Introvert

Key words: *communication, easy friendship, relaxation, creativity, social influence, difficulty in focusing, dispersion*

The *extroverted behavior person* seems to live intensely, having three basic needs: recognition, connection, and communication. People under this archetype have their feelings stamped on their faces; they have difficulty hiding what they think and feel, whether it's happiness, sadness, worry, or tranquillity. As much as they try to demonstrate otherwise, everything about *extroverts* reflect their state of mind: the tone of voice, the speed of speech, the colors of their clothes, the body language.

Do you know the kind of person who is always starting something new but almost never finishes the previous task? Who has a new idea every moment but in the next doesn't quite remember what it was? That even as an adult has the vivacity of a child—and stubbornness, too? This is the extrovert!

People governed by an *extroverted behavior Odu* need constant encouragement and validation. They get bored quickly and expect compliments all the time, even if they often don't know how to receive them. They are communicative and charismatic and have the ability to persuade through speech and the use of words. Born optimists, they always see the positive side of any situation. Therefore, every event is a reason for celebration and enthusiasm as if it were the biggest achievement of all! However, as they are extremely emotional, when something bothers them, they tend to experience pain and sadness in the same intensity.

Regarding social relationships, the extroverted behavior is influential and makes friends easily, being extremely flexible in socializing with other people, which facilitates their adaptation to different scenarios in life. Most of them are highly creative and versatile people, with great skills in group work and in reconciling crises and conflicts.

However, due to all the excitement and enthusiasm that are characteristic of them, they fail in planning and in the logical interpretation of situations, and they can still devote themselves to pursuing an unfeasible goal simply because they believe in it, without observing the surrounding reality. With all of this, when the negative aspect of this regency presents itself, in addition to the lack of critical analysis, those governed by an *introverted behavior Odu* are resistant to obeying rules and following processes, norms, and schedules. In this same sense, introverted behavior people have great difficulty meeting deadlines and keeping focused on tasks and situations that require effort that is more practical than creative.

Analytical/Hesitant

Key words: *caution, quality, demand, accuracy, calculations and spreadsheets, detail, perfection, high level of demand*

The *analytical behavior person* is always thinking and planning and, therefore, has two basic needs: to be correct (which does not necessarily mean to be right as in dominant behavior but *to be exact*) and to do things the right way, following standards, rules, and defined processes. Consequently, the main characteristic of analytical behavior is caution and planning, which, in turn, means that one always ends up identifying and worrying about the negative side of situations, with the intention of preventing them from happening.

Do you know that person who every time a new idea or project comes up immediately asks, "But what if?" Who always has a consideration or criticism to make, seeking unattainable perfection in everything? Who is always taking notes and creating to-do lists for even the simplest of everyday things? This is the analytical.

People governed by an *analytical behavior Odu* are extremely organized and detail oriented, sometimes bordering on neurotic perfectionism. Meticulous and constantly concerned, they value constant planning; to live in peace, they need to establish well-defined and repetitive routines and processes.

The analytical behavior people are extremely observant and base their perceptions and decisions on logic and on what can be seen in numbers, calculations, and spreadsheets. They have a great capacity for focus and concentration and only rest after finishing a task, even if the result does not match their expectations. They are inflexible *while carrying out processes* but highly flexible and adaptable *once they reach a conclusion* about facts and situations. Analytical people are able to develop logical connections and reasoning that others would never imagine.

Analytical behavior people also do not tolerate any pressure or demands that would force them to deviate from a plan; they find it very difficult to adapt to changes and unforeseen events. They are very resistant to criticism, once they have done the work and reached their objective. They speak little, but when they do, they demonstrate knowledge and authority in their words; in the same way, they are righteous and true people by nature.

In its negative aspect, however, analytical behavior is called *hesitant behavior.* After so much thinking, planning, researching, and searching, they end up theorizing so much that they find several possible answers and solutions for any given situation and, therefore, resist choosing only one as the most correct. This is the main personality trait of the hesitant, and although it seems to be related to the objective and concrete aspects of daily life, it especially applies to subjective and emotional issues.

Indecision is also part of this behavior, as well as little practicality. When the downside of this behavioral style occurs, it is common for the hesitant behavior person to spend a lot of time on activities that do not require as much care or attention, reviewing and rethinking the obvious. It is also common for the hesitant person to have difficulties in making decisions or giving directions. Analytical people are not good at self-direction and do better as followers than in leadership roles. This tendency is even more clear and constant in personal relationships. Analytical/hesitant people always want to discuss the relationship; they always have something to correct in themselves or in others and are always ready to give their constructive criticisms.

Patient/Impatient

Key words: *stability, conciliation, balance, temperance, tranquillity, harmony, responsibility*

Patient behavior people put the needs of others before their own, often harming themselves to care for someone else. Excellent advisers, their opinions convey confidence even in the face of challenges, and they have two main needs: security and harmony.

Do you know that kind of person who always seems to be at peace, even when the worst situation presents itself? Who speaks and acts as if no commitment is as important as living the present fully? Who hardly gives his opinion about situations but listens to everything and everyone and accepts the decisions that are taken in the best way possible? This is the *patient*.

Like analytical behavior people, those governed by a *patient behavior Odu* tend to plan a lot and love routine, but for different reasons. While analytical people seek the most correct and fair result, the patient behavior people eat the same breakfast every day, take the same route from home to work, or engage in the same leisure activities as tools to meet their need for safety and balance.

In the same way, in social and love relationships, patient behavior people—which could very well be called *pacifist behavior*—avoid any kind of conflict, even if it is necessary to remain silent and abstain from their wishes or opinions. Silence, by the way, is one of their greatest features! In the same way, they are always willing to help and advise those who seek them out. Stable and conservative, they find it difficult to adapt to changes and therefore seek to live at a steady pace and tend to keep long-term relationships that last several years.

Patient behavior people work well as a team and seem to live in constant balance, getting average results in practically everything they set out to do. Easy to get along with and highly trustworthy, they tend to have a good sense of justice, excelling at managing conflicts and identifying positive and negative points about themselves, other people, or tasks that need to be optimized and improved.

On the negative side, *impatient behavior* makes them intransigent and extremely stubborn people, with a low ability to improvise when necessary and limited creativity because they cling to defined and established routines. In this aspect, they also demonstrate difficulty in innovation and little or no sense of urgency and priorities: they can postpone the completion of tasks and situations because they feel they need to be revised or replanned.

In addition, those governed by impatient behavior are also highly pessimistic and possessive, even tending to keep secrets and hide results, which directly interferes with their ability to socialize. Broadening the interpretation of these characteristics, the negative influences of *impatient behavior Odus* become dangerous and can sometimes lead to complete stagnation of life and desires. In these situations, the intervention of someone with dominant behavior is necessary to get them out of this scenario.

◖ What Is Your Style?

Based on the descriptions of the four behavioral styles and from how you see yourself at this point in life, which one best defines your personality?

( ) Dominant

( ) Extroverted

( ) Analytical

( ) Patient

INTERPRETATIONS OF BIRTH ODUS

Next, you will learn how the sixteen Odus are classified and interpreted, including their number, motto that defines them, vibration, element of nature, and behavior. Furthermore, the text after their list of characteristics is an example of how they would be interpreted on a birth chart assessment.

Okaran

Number: 1
Motto: The dangers of the world are always spreading
Vibration: Female
Element of Nature: Earth/Water
Behavior: Extroverted/Impulsive

Okaran is the Odu that rules everyone and no one simultaneously and never occupies a Orishas birth chart position. After all, we are all subject to the dangers of the world, the fears of destiny, and, especially, the consequences of the choices and decisions that, right or wrong, we make every day.

Master of contrasts, it is this Odu that commands the risks and the inevitable catastrophes as well as the great salvations and conquests. Okaran calls for caution, attention, care, and precaution: Eshu is the owner of all paths and crossroads, and pleasing him is a must for these paths to be gentle and light, which is exactly how life should be. With this, despite the constant threats, Okaran teaches us that one cannot take a step without taking risks. To be aware of it while facing and overcoming faith with courage is the greatest mission for our personal evolution.

Those who have Eshu's protection are more likely not to come across Okaran's surprises. More than that, it is through Eshu's blessings that victories are ensured—after all, what he gives, only he can take away.

Ejioko

Number: 2
Motto: The joy of life is seen through the eyes of innocence
Vibration: Female
Element of Nature: Earth/Air
Behavior: Extroverted/Impulsive

Key Expressions

Positive	Negative
Destined for success	Temperamental
Generous	Disobeys rules
Above-average intelligence	Stubborn and insistent
Artistic and creative	Uncompromising
Avant-garde personality	Has difficulty finishing things
	Problems in pregnancy or childbirth
	Naive

Ah! You'd like life to always be a party, wouldn't you? For those who, like you, were born conquering death, every moment is celebrated as if there were no tomorrow. The sparkle in your eyes dazzles those who see them, and you go through life with vivacity, with an intelligence and creativity that are above average. Rest assured: you were born for success!

The creative intelligence and versatility that are peculiar to you make you always want the new, and you seek out the countless options that the world has to offer. Always curious, when you see a new opportunity on the horizon, you quickly make your way toward it, trying it out, and even, for a short time, delighting yourself with everything it has to offer.

Although it can be delicious tasting all the flavors that life has to offer, you must learn to identify which opportunities really serve you and are good for you. Naive by nature, with an urge to discover and explore, you may end up getting involved in situations that are not the best for you but only realize this after it's too late. All this excitement of discovery and your vivacious disposition need to be balanced with a little rationality and maturity.

Anxiety and childlike innocence are your enemies—two weaknesses that you must work hard to conquer. The world is fraught with dangers that, if you insist on wearing your armor like a character in a fantasy story, you won't be able to defeat. The world is harder than it looks, and people will sometimes hurt you—even if you are incapable of hurting them.

Often ingenious and disobedient, you do not accept the advice of your elders and bosses, and therefore, you end up taking long and winding paths out of sheer stubbornness. This also makes you give up on your goals halfway through, and that is why *persistence* should be the key word in all your endeavors.

Your great intelligence and inventive capacity make you stand out from the rest, but this can cause you to feel and act superior toward others; that, combined with your strong and inflexible genius, can end up creating disaffection and alienating you from the people around you. As you naturally prefer in avant-garde life situations, you find it difficult to balance your desire for innovation with the need to accept others' differences and limitations—yours and theirs.

Still, you are destinated for brilliance and resilience! Therefore, the sooner you learn to balance the joy that makes you always smile with the demands of adult life, the sooner you will start to experience the success and plenitude that the universe has to offer.

Eta-Ogunda or Ogunda

Number: 3
Motto: The battle road is the one that leads to victory
Vibration: Male
Element of Nature: Fire, air
Behavior: Analytical, impulsive

Key Expressions

Positive	Negative
Virile and fertile	Authoritarian
Strategic intelligence	Stubborn
Pioneering	Tendency to lie
Proactive and inquisitive	Difficulty in taking responsibility
Hardworking	Always saying "it wasn't me"
Communicative	Jealous and possessive
Easily changes everything (place, friends, partner	Tendency toward depression

For you, the world is a battleground, and war seems to be eternal. Intelligent and pioneering, you keep wondering if you're fighting the good fight and, with that, put even more doubts and difficulties on a path that, by itself, would not be easy.

The regency of Odu Ogunda makes you an extremely intelligent and strategic person. You are always making plans, setting and pursuing goals. In your thoughts, the impossible seems just a matter of a little more effort to become reality. However, one of the most delicate aspects is balancing pride and efficiency. Although it is satisfying to look at an achievement and think, "I did all that," it is important to recognize that a lot has already been thought out, planned and created: you don't need to reinvent the wheel with each new goal you want to achieve.

At this point it's quite possible that you're thinking either "I'm not like that" or "That's just the way I am"—and, well, that's just one more proof that this almost authoritarian stubbornness in always doing things your way is true.

You are an incredibly curious and inquisitive person, and it's time to use this great quality to your advantage. A pioneer by nature, there are no closed paths for you. You're usually the first to raise your hand and say, "Let me do it"—if you haven't already started to do it while others are still thinking about it. This pioneering spirit, combined with your unique communication skills, is what makes you stand out from the crowd.

However, these same characteristics can torment you. The ease with which you start things is not proportional with your ability to finish them: you always end up leaving some plans unfinished and overloading yourself, mentally and emotionally. This emotional weight and the difficulty you have in dealing with frustrations ends up enhancing the negative aspects of Odu Ogunda, giving rise to aggressiveness.

Have you ever considered that you are also entitled to peace? All this demand that you put upon yourself does not end well, and you carry within you a silent sadness that can easily turn into depression. Focus and determination are your key words, and if you concentrate on a single activity, you will easily reach success, but if you try to do everything at the same time, you will undoubtedly get lost along the way.

Iorossun

> Number: 4
> Motto: The head carries the body
> Vibration: Male
> Element of Nature: Fire/Earth
> Behavior: Dominant/Hesitant

Key Expressions

Positive	Negative
Analytical intelligence	Authoritarian
Great reasoning ability	Aggressive when speaking
Skill with words (especially writing)	Stands alone in the crowd
Quick thinking	Relationship issues with the mother
Good adviser	Tendency to take responsibility for the problems of others
Eloquent and well spoken	
	Thinks a lot and acts little, leading to stagnation
	Serious illnesses with a spiritual background

Thinking, reflecting, studying, meditating—intelligence is your greatest virtue. But what good comes from knowing everything about all the sciences and having all the knowledge in the world if you get lost and stagnate before putting it into practice?

Your generosity and ability with words make you a good counselor; since childhood your friends and family have sought you for your wise and prompt guidance. This, however, also makes you tend to take on the role of everyone's mother or father, absorbing the problems of others as your own.

It is necessary to find balance and know how to take responsibility only for what is yours, allowing others to take responsibility for what is theirs. Who said you should save the world?

You absorb every image, every word, every piece of information you encounter and internally create connections between them and the reality around you—symbols and meanings, icons and contexts. It seems that, with so much to learn and teach, your mind never rests, even when your body asks for some time to itself. A word spoken to you at the right time or a small new idea spontaneously occurring to you can cause a revolution in your thoughts, and you automatically enter an inner world until, from there, a grandiose project emerges, and you immediately take it forward with everything you've just (re)discovered.

Aware that your path is lonely, you are always ready to help anyone who comes to you as long as this help does not jeopardize your natural freedom and independence. Communication is your great tool, but it can also be your lethal weapon, as you can use your tongue like a whip and can't keep secrets for long.

Faith and awareness of yourself, your qualities, and your limitations make you a great thinker, and your path is always based on rationality and stability. Inquisitive, you need absolute answers, definitions, and immutable certainties to feel secure. With all this, the problem is that after thinking so much, you tend to get isolated in your plans and thoughts. Proud of your intellectual capabilities, no idea goes public without you being sure it's the *best* idea (in your opinion). If someone contradicts you, you see it as an act of ignorance, and you are willing to fight for your idea until you become the winner. But—would you rather be happy or right?

Oshe

Number: 5

Motto: The shine of gold fascinates and dazzles

Vibration: Male

Element of Nature: Air/Air

Behavior: Extroverted/Hesitant

Key Expressions

Positive	Negative
Charming and elegant	Malicious
Attracts fame	Tendency to lie, pretend, and dissimulate
Has good taste and refinement	Emotionally dependent
Ability to easily generate wealth and earn money	Greedy
	Jealous and vindictive
Loving and sentimental	Spiteful, difficulty forgiving
Ingenious, knows how to create plans and execute them	
Proactive	

You attract glances wherever you go and, full of charm and beauty, walk through life like a model on a catwalk. You love a mirror, good jewelry, a nice outfit, and a good bank account—yours and whoever is by your side; after all, you were not born to live with less than the best.

Being the center of attention and occupying prominent positions has become commonplace for you. You have a propensity to succeed in whatever area you choose to work in; however, it is important to be aware that not all looks cast your way are of praise and recognition. Your glow and charisma make you absorb the negative energies of places and people, and you are often the target of envy and persecution—rivals who give you a kiss on the cheek, while stabbing you in the back. However, this is a setback you need to get used to, as it's a low price to pay for the natural notoriety and recognition that is part of your personality.

Without much effort you make yourself seen and wanted. Your refined taste attracts attention and, combined with your ease of earning money, puts you in contact with wealthy social circles—which you should take advantage of, since through social contagion you can reach an even higher position than the one you already have (and you have plenty of sympathy and charisma for that).

The heart, however, is your weak point, and it is possible to say that you are only OK when you are with someone, isn't it? In fact, you often prefer to live unhappily with someone else than to seek happiness alone. Loneliness frightens you as the night frightens a child—and that's how you've been treating your relationships. If brightness and beauty guide your steps, it is love that makes you deviate from your goals. Love feeds and torments you, and without it you would not know how to live. You enjoy the game of love, pretending to disdain the affections of another and playing games of dissimulation; however, you rage and lose balance when rejected—which is usually because you push your games to the limit. This emotional dependency is your lot, and you often act like you're addicted to lamentation and in love with feeling pain.

The key to victory in every aspect of your life is learning to use your intuition and your personal magic: this is the power the Orishas have given you, and learning to work the potential of these spiritual gifts will make you discover that life is unlimited and that happiness and abundance are at your disposal. Stop complaining, roll up your sleeves, and seek the best that the world has for you.

Obara

Number: 6
Motto: Money can't buy happiness
Vibration: Male
Element of Nature: Air/Earth
Behavior: Extroverted/Impulsive

Key Expressions

Positive	Negative
Natural beauty	Lack of initiative
Charismatic	Uncompromising
Humorous	Proud
Easily makes friends	Talks too much and doesn't listen to people
Skillful with sales and money	Naive, trusts too much
Good money administrator	Tendency to lie and fantasize
Great sales abilities	Tendency to depression, especially due to childhood trauma

Your charisma defines you, and your smile illuminates the places you pass through and enchants everyone around you. No wonder you make friends quickly, as you were born to share joy and good humor with the world. However, naïveté and intransigence are also striking factors in your personality, which can transform this entire beautiful scene into a canvas of affliction and sadness.

A good salesperson and a good manager—especially of other people's money—you are convinced that it is the management of physical and spiritual resources that leads to growth and wealth. This management ability is one of your best features, which can transform you into a rich and prosperous person in a short time. The big problem, however, is that results only come when ideas leave the paper and become action. You flirt with so many ideas at the same time that you drain yourself of the energy and initiative needed to move any one of them forward; you need to look inside yourself and take the necessary steps to put your boldest goals into practice.

Furthermore, you need to understand that no one is an island and that journeying alone is always more difficult. Despite being very communicative, your excessive pride and naïveté in wanting to do everything your way prevents you from asking for help, which makes it difficult for you to carry out your plans. Consequently, you flirt with depression, especially when present situations bring memories of traumas experienced in childhood.

We live in the real world, and even with the regency of Odu Obara favoring your destiny, difficulties will knock at your door from time to time. When these moments come, it is important to remember that you will be forced to face your difficulties whether you like it or not; otherwise, you risk immersing yourself in a fantasy world. So why not try easing your way through them? With this in mind, you will have to recognize that you have been lying to yourself, which is the worst kind of lie, and this recognition will destroy the fairy tale you have so carefully designed to defend yourself from the traumas of the past. Life is good, and you deserve to enjoy it, without mistakes. Fairy tales, after all, are just fantasy.

However, this does not mean that you should accept everything and everyone who comes forward. With your tendency to trust people too much—which will inevitably bring you disappointments that can only be overcome with balance and judgment—the key to your evolution is to learn who and why to trust each person who enters your life.

Odi

Number: 7

Motto: There is no easy way when pain comes from the heart

Vibration: Female

Element of Nature: Air/Water

Behavior: Patient/Impulsive

Key Expressions

Positive	Negative
Analytical intelligence	Does not tolerate weakness and incompetence
Persistent and persevering	
Good memory, remembers even the smallest details	Engages in gossip
	Has difficulty keeping secrets
Hard worker	Marital infidelity
Careful and zealous about activities and relationships	Superstitious
	Doubts everything and everyone
Always seeks excellence and perfection	Unyielding
	Jealous
	Lonely, prefers to live isolated from people

The weight of the world seems light in comparison with what you carry in your heart. It is not easy to bear so much pain while wearing a smile on your face and trying, every day, to be happy—or to at least look like you are. You have been facing challenges since you came into the world, and it seems that with every step a new challenge arises. Unfortunately, this is the nature of the reality you live in!

It seems that everything is more difficult for you, and you always have the impression that, even when the way in front of you seems straightfoward and smooth, the universe always puts obstacles in your path to distract you and demands that you face difficulties that, until then, didn't even exist. But if you think about it—and we need to be honest here—most of the time it's you who creates these obstacles by doubting your own ability.

However, with all the weight carried until now, you can already consider yourself a winner. Nobody in the world has your stamina and willpower; after all, "to persist where anyone else would give up" is your way and motto of living! Not giving up is the key to your victory—and I guarantee you, it will come true. But always remember: the universe reflects back to us whatever we project onto it, and given the pessimism that is natural to you, the setbacks you encounter are nothing more than reflections of your thoughts.

However, care must be taken to avoid creating expectations greater than reality can provide. You already know the misadventures of the steps you tread, and that is why it is important to know how to measure and balance how much demand you put on yourself and others. In the pursuit of perfection, you may find it difficult to meet the desired and required level of quality, and as a result, you will inevitably suffer from frustration.

In addition, having learned through life to withstand the pains and hardships of fate, you are often inflexibile and stubborn in the face of problems. Full of superstition, jealousy, and possessiveness about everything and everyone with whom you relate ends up driving away those who love you, as they feel suffocated with your dominating character. In fact, they don't realize that this is your way of showing how much you care and are afraid of losing them, but unfortunately, behaving this way ends up making life a lonely journey.

Your feeling of emptiness in the soul and your past experiences make your heart ache. But know that everyone encounters exactly the challenges they are capable of withstanding. With all the stones your life has thrown at you, believe me, you can build a beautiful and grand castle, and your way can become lighter when you have someone by your side to give you a hand when the pain seems too great. How about giving it a try?

Ejiogbe

Number: 8
Motto: The tongue is the whip of the body
Vibration: Male
Element of Nature: Fire/Fire
Behavior: Analytical/Impulsive

Key Expressions

Positive	Negative
Able to socialize for politics	Gets sick of things easily
Eloquent	Ethics and morals flexible to the interests of the moment
Great speaker, knows how to speak and convince	
	Experiences violent passions
Able to perform multiple tasks at the same time	Impulsive and vindictive
	Tendency to pretend and lie
Looks for excellence	Favors intrigue for the pleasure of watching it
Ambitious	
Curious and inquisitive	Lives surrounded by confusion and falsehood

In the game of life, no one is a match for you. A natural-born politician (although you are often perverse), you can identify the subtlest nuances of the reality around you and use each one of them to your advantage, no matter who gets hurt. Extremely intelligent, sometimes even Machiavellian, you devise and execute complex plans to achieve your goals in all areas of life.

When you're good, you are the best. When you're bad, you're the worst. Your ambitious personality makes you achieve excellence in everything you propose. Master of subtle wars, you live in doubt about yourself and the world, and these inner conflicts often haunt you and can make you lose sleep, but you have enough skill to hide negative thoughts and feelings from yourself.

You always seek perfection and demand the same from the people around you. Your skills at reasoning and critical analysis make you an excellent manager and architect of great projects and strategies—for better and for worse. In fact, it is on this razor's edge that you trace your way through life: good and evil are relative to you, and your interests are molded to circumstances. Duality is a figure present in your daily life, and curiosity can be your ally or your tormentor.

You have desires for power and knowledge about everything and everyone. Likewise, you usually don't consider the consequences of reaching your goals and, sometimes, end up compromising your values and taking advantage of people to get where you want. This, however, haunts you every day and reflects the great doubts that exist within you. Instead of always looking outside, how about look inside yourself and realize that you are capable and deserving of reaching your goals and can be victorious without needing to hurt anyone, even when circumstances suggest you need to do otherwise?

To appease your soul's conflicts, you need to be the first to believe in yourself, sincerely and honestly. Only then will the people around you truly recognize your worth and no longer agree with you just to avoid getting you angry; otherwise, they risk your fury because you see disagreement as a betrayal.

You tend to easily get bored with things, and in a split second they lose their grace and charm, becoming more of the same. It is precisely from this mediocrity that you flee, and against it that you fight hard, often creating fanciful realities to justify your attitudes and hide the truth that hurts your soul: even if, in your heart, you believe you are a king, you must learn to govern before you can wear the crown.

Ossa

Number: 9

Motto: Fire and passion running through your veins

Vibration: Female

Element of Nature: Water/Fire

Behavior: Dominant/Impulsive

Key Expressions

Positive	Negative
Strategic intelligence	Overbearing and arrogant
Generous	Doesn't listen to anyone and talks too much
Tireless worker	Lives surrounded by false friends
Great willpower	Suffers from the persecution of women
Friendly and charismatic	Impulsive, takes all feelings to the extreme
Benevolent	
Does not hold grudges or grievances	Despairs if things are not done his or her way
Very clairvoyant and intuitive	Tendency to have multiple relationships

You are full of fire and intensity. A small spark in the air and you can generate a great explosion of feelings, desires, and passions of all kinds. Generous and benevolent, yet authoritative and demanding with others and with yourself, you carry in your chest all the untimeliness of the world.

You tend to speak and act without thinking, saying whatever comes to mind without listening to anyone. Then you run to put out the fire that you started yourself, all because you wanted the world to keep up with you—which, between us, will hardly ever happen.

Your intelligence and willpower, allied to the courage and capacity to perform and produce far beyond average, are what move you and give you the courage to keep going forward, facing everything and everyone. However, be careful because so much fire can burn everything to ashes and leave you alone amid the hurt caused along the way. Whoever hits forgets, but whoever gets beaten always remembers, and with your tongue, sincerity can turn into cruelty.

Freedom is your driving force, and any person or situation that dares to prevent you from moving forward with the speed of the wind will be easily discarded by your heart, which beats strongly with the desire to conquer and dominate everything: people, places, goals. You move mountains for what you love. However, it is these same passions that make you take situations to the extreme and cause you to experience a roller coaster of feelings every day.

Because of the daring that is peculiar to you, people recognize you wherever you go. "Who is that, so full of herself, defeating lions and conquering new territories every day?" they ask! And so, you follow your path of conquests and success, marked by the courage to break new horizons and overcome the bad weather and storms of the world, even if you must pay the price of loneliness. In addition, you need to be aware of women persecuting you in every area of your life, who will continually conflict and quarrel with you, even if you don't realize it or don't dislike them.

Learning to balance reason and emotion, and understanding that while your voice, advice, and opinions are always heard, they are not the only ones that deserve attention and recognition—this is the key to happiness. I know you don't do any of this out of malice; on the contrary, there is a fire burning in your chest, and this is what makes you intense and urgent, but remember the same fire that warms can also ignite.

Ofun

Number: 10
Motto: Time is the lord of reason
Vibration: Female
Element of Nature: Water/Water
Behavior: Patient/Hesitant

Key Expressions

Positive	Negative
Patient and understanding	Proud, doesn't accept being forced into anything
Consolidates material goods	
Creates and maintains long-term friendships and relationships	Resistance to renounce the past
	Stubborn and unyielding
Airs of authority	Jealous and possessive
Generous	Has great difficulty finishing things
Great word skills, especially spoken	Carries the faults of the world in the soul
Intelligent and eloquent	
Tendency to live many years	Absorbs anger, somatizing in the body

Oh if everyone in the world had your calm and uprightness! Your greatest power is in your voice—that you speak and shut up at the right time and in the exact measure. Likewise, understanding yourself and others seems to be the path to enlightenment, and you've been working on this since childhood, when you already seemed more mature than others.

All this knowledge, wisdom, and experience, however, fan your pride and arrogance, which often ignites a flame of tyranny within you. As a result, you become inflexible and intolerant of other people's will and opinions, not accepting that they also have experiences from which you can learn.

Optimistic by nature, you believe that despite all the difficulties, the future will always be better than today. In fact, the ability to deal with the most complex situations with the understanding and tranquillity of someone who has acquired wisdom throughout life is one of your greatest qualities.

Nothing seems to shake you, and even amid the biggest storms, you always maintain an understanding and considerate vibe, giving yourself fully to the current moment. Dreamy, you know exactly where you want to go, just as you know the way there will be long and tiring. For this reason, you often give up halfway through the journey and leave your plans and projects unfinished.

Despite such apparent calm and humbleness, you carry a great tyrant within you and do not accept being forced into anything; otherwise, in a fit of fury, you abandon whatever you are doing. You were created to command and not to be commanded, but that inflexibility and stubbornness, crippled by the excessive pride you try to hide under a polite smile, can become your worst enemies if you don't find the balance between giving and receiving. What about trying to keep in mind that even if things don't go your way, they can wisely end according to your wishes?

Your attachment to the past is the main point that prevents the fulfillment of your inner revolution, to what the key is to exercise forgiveness and absolve yourself of the guilt you carry hidden in your heart! Having the weight of the world on your back has already become routine for you, but it is precisely this weight—which, by the way, does not belong to you—that slows you down and makes the true transformation of your destiny take longer to happen.

Owarin

Number: 11

Motto: Only lonely paths do not bring discord

Vibration: Female

Element of Nature: Earth/Fire

Behavior: Dominant/Introverted

Key Expressions

Positive	Negative
Communicative, makes friends easily	Victim of slander, betrayals, ingratitude, and scams
Tendency to acquire wealth in youth	Experiences constant nervousness
	Has difficulty saying no
Ability to start over from scratch, like the Phoenix	Risk of spiritual illnesses and death in youth
Good heart	Lives with persecution and imbalances caused by relationships with three or more people
Born entrepreneur	
Natural beauty and good luck	
Brave and stubborn, pursues goals at any price	

How good it is to be able to recognize that, despite everything, good luck accompanies you even in the biggest storms! Your self-confidence, determination, and obstinacy to achieve your goals are your trademark attributes. It is with this feeling that you wake up every day and make a point of pursuing your goals from a young age; after all, tomorrow is always an uncertainty for you.

You live every second to the extreme, at a speed that only you can follow and execute. You don't expect anything from anyone and prefer to pay the price to pay to see it. Such agility and speed, however, make you an extremely irritable person: the world doesn't seem to be prepared to happen as quickly as you would like. This affects you deeply, especially on an emotional level, causing chronic and excessive nervousness that can often be reflected in the body through psychosomatic illnesses. You have an urge to live, to achieve, and to conquer, as if you were sure that death is waiting to take you at any time—and if so, you'll be make sure you have fulfilled your goals and enjoyed this life to the fullest.

With a good heart, you're generous and easily earn and manage money, especially in your youth. Unfortunately, however, you also have a great difficulty saying no to anyone who asks for help, and this often makes you an easy victim for scams. As our elders teach, "to do good without looking comes at a high cost." You need to learn this hard lesson; otherwise, you will suffer from the ingratitude even of those closest to you, who, no matter how much help they get, will always say that you didn't do more than your duty. Remember that you first need to take care of yourself; by looking too much at the outer world, you have repeatedly forgotten about your inner world and the strength you have.

Your ability to reinvent yourself at every moment, rising from the ashes like the Phoenix, growing stronger and more beautiful, make you even more attractive, and you get attention wherever you go. The self-confidence that is peculiar to you inspires people around you, who look at you and, even without being able to explain it, realize that there is something special and positive in your aura. Add to that your exceptional business acumen, communication skills, and ease with making friends, and you've got the world at your feet.

Ejilaxebora

Number: 12
Motto: Justice is equality among equals
Vibration: Male
Element of Nature: Water/Air
Behavior: Analytical/Hesitant

Key Expressions

Positive	Negative
Sociable and communicative	Noisy and explosive
Politeness	Vain
Great skill with the written word	Tends to have multiple partners
Diplomatic and persuasive	Dreamer, has difficulties in acting
Intriguing and seductive	Tendency to lie and spread falsehood
Great ability to perceive the nuances of the surrounding reality	Proud, if contradicted becomes authoritarian and arrogant

Those destined to royalty will never lack its majesty, and your haughty and diplomatic personality, along with the way you look and walk, makes you a queen par excellence. Politic, diplomatic, and well spoken, you enchant the people around you, even though what you say is not always what you really feel. Sincerity and truth, for you, do not go hand in hand.

You are intriguing and arouse passions wherever you go. Persuasive, skilled with the written word, and with a great perceptive abilities, you know how to identify the most discreet behavioral and relationship nuances, and that is why you do very well in hierarchical careers, in which you will certainly grow and reach high positions. By the way, here's something that delights you: titles and high rank, which feed your vanity and inflate your ego—and that's also where the danger lies.

Like the crown of your personal reign, arrogance easily goes to the head. With this, what could be used as a lever for success ends up becoming a hindrance in your personality. These same aspects can also make you explosive, noisy, and selfish, especially when your wishes are not immediately met. As you believe yourself to be above good and evil, you end up flirting with tyranny, and instead of being liked, you become feared by the people around you.

Friendly and well spoken, you make allies easily but have great difficulties in maintaining long-term friendships—often due to the daily commitments and tasks for which you take responsibility. Still, it is normal—and even expected—for you to dream big and, in these dreams, project hopes and expectations onto other people, as if they had an obligation to follow in your footsteps and pursue your goals as if they were theirs. But things aren't exactly like that, and forcing reality to fit your dreams can make you your own tormentor.

Each soul has its own paths, desires, and capabilities. That's why it's important to learn early on that your ambitions are uniquely yours. As much as it is possible and often necessary to rely on others to fulfill your desires, you need to balance your pride and understand that, if within you there is a crown, its brilliance is not always perceived and recognized beyond yourself. In that case, leadership and authoritarianism can get mixed up and bring you heartbreak and defeat. Learning to lead and govern, meeting the needs of others without hurting your own will, is the key to your success.

Ojiologbon

Number: 13

Mote: In life, we all die slowly every day

Vibration: Female

Element of Nature: Earth/Earth

Behavior: Patient/Introvert

Key Expressions

Positive	Negative
Fair and honest	Impressionable and influenceable
Excellent adviser	Strong in public but cries alone
Docile and kind	Talks too much and doesn't keep secrets
Good taste but prefers simple things	Gets involved in issues that do not concern them
Accumulates knowledge, knows a little bit about everything	Emotionally dependent
Prefers to live in a group rather than alone	

You are a source of wisdom and inspiration to people, even if you have enormous difficulties in recognizing your own value and potential. Wise, fair, and sincere, you perform with excellence the role of adviser and comforter to those who suffer a loss; however, you also end up hurting yourself by putting aside your own feelings to take care of others.

With your words and your gentle manner, you have the power to renew people's hopes so that they trust the greater good and continue to live. How about, then, starting to listen to your own advice and practice it in your life?

You prefer the simple things in life and have great difficulty dealing with moments of solitude, preferring to live in groups. This is because the fear of death is strengthened when you find yourself alone, with your thoughts, in a reverie. However, the biggest conflict is that the constant coexistence in groups is allied to the difficulty in assuming and defending your own opinions, afraid to hurt or lose someone's affection by saying what you think. To please everyone around you—and precisely because of the ability to understand and reconcile different opinions—you end up becoming influenceable and impressionable.

All the news in the world interests you, and with that, you accumulate knowledge. There isn't a single subject in life that you haven't already heard about and wanted to know about. The problem is that it also extends to subjects about other people's lives, which you can hardly keep to yourself.

So as not to get upset with anyone and maintain a good relationship with all people, you prefer that your decisions are made by other people, so that you can avoid taking responsibility for your own choices. This can make things seem easier, but it is important to understand to what extent this attitude of yours is not, in fact, a way to escape the demands that life imposes and, with that, strengthen the hurts and pains you insist on internalizing.

Despite all this, the time has come to accept that you are also human and have the right to cry. I know you hide your own pain by feeling obligated to always appear strong and victorious, but the inner hurts you've been accumulating throughout your life are silently hurting you and this needs to stop. Believe me: you have great inner strength! This needs to be worked on urgently; after all, a wounded soul quickly turns into an emotionally sick body, which will certainly somatize the inner pains into physical wounds.

Ika

Number: 14

Motto: Everything in the world is eternal until it comes to an end

Vibration: Male

Element of Nature: Water/Earth

Behavior: Analytical/Impulsive

Key Expressions

Positive	Negative
Confident and self-assured	Dramatic, gravitates toward superlative situations
Ability to create good friendships	
Predisposition to heroism	Has personality antagonisms
Courageous, does not hesitate in the face of danger	Impulsive, takes everything to the extreme
Ease of accumulating wealth and prosperity	Has difficulty trusting others
	Traumas due to physical and sexual violence
Material detachment and generosity	

How much willpower and how much willingness! Your destiny is a path of constant revolution. You've not only gotten used to it, you miss it when, from time to time, your life doesn't turn upside down and demands that you be reborn as a Phoenix from the ashes.

Active and insightful, you are the typical citizen of the world: you do not belong anywhere, and at the same time you belong everywhere.

If you could, you would even be in all places at the same time. Your ability to get in and out of any situation—as well as to make yourself noticed in each of them—guarantees you a prominent position in whatever you do. However, like the wheel of life, in a short time you get tired of what is set, and an urgent and overwhelming desire makes you walk, travel, grow, and change.

However, such urgency for change can often prevent you from sticking to a single activity as you constantly change jobs and don't create a consolidated professional history. Therefore, it is important that you find the balance between the flame that burns within you and that you want to project to the world and the demands of real life, which will often ask for a little patience and stability so that you can reap good results in the future.

Your social skills, however, are often hampered by the difficulty you have in trusting people. Therefore, it is necessary to know how to differentiate the people in your social circle and in your professional circle, what role each of them plays in your life, and what role you play in each of theirs. By answering these questions, you will surely find the balance point to give your best and get the same in return without having to give up your individuality and privacy.

Infinity is your horizon, and nothing can stop you. However, you must understand that not everyone around you is willing to continually reinvent themselves, and many are looking for solidity and stability, which, at this rate, you will unfortunately not be able to offer. All this impulsiveness that is natural to you can end up generating conflicts with the people you care about and even create difficulties in establishing lasting bonds, such as a marriage or a career at a single company.

During so many revolutions per second, it might be a good idea to stop for a moment and reflect on what your priorities are and where, exactly, you want to go. The inconstancy, even if positive, often makes you lose or give up opportunities, people, and situations that are right at your side and that can, very well, supply this urge to overcome yourself at every moment.

Obeogunda

Number: 15

Motto: The force that moves is the same that paralyzes

Vibration: Male

Element of Nature: Fire/Water

Behavior: Dominant/Impulsive

Key Expressions

Positive	Negative
Courageous	Extremist
Hardworker	Uncompromising
Audacious	Tendency to depression and madness
Always searches for the new	
	Lonely
Helpful and willing	
	Undisciplined
Carries an internal desire for conquest	
	Jealous, has violent relationships

How courageous and daring you are! The intensity and inconstancy of your choices clearly demonstrate that you are guided by the need to conquer the impossible and transform the reality around you according to your will, never taking into consideration the effort necessary or the consequences.

A provider by nature, work is what gives you the courage to move forward, against everything that tries to prevent you from always moving ahead, seeking new horizons and new goals. This desire for conquest applies as much to your desires as to the desires and dreams of those you care about. The problem, however, is that they're not always (or rather, almost never) at the same pace as you, and for that reason, it's hard to keep your loved ones around. This can often make group interactions and social relations difficult, and in an increasingly plural and globalized world, it is important to learn to relate better with people.

By the way, living the paths of excess and extremes can easily lead to addictions, including addiction to work or toxic relationships. Due to so many contrasts, it is necessary to learn once and for all that although not everyone around you can be considered friends, they also do not need to be branded as opponents of war. Guided by excess, fire, and passion for what you do, you take all your feelings to the extreme. There are no compromises, and for you everything seems to be lived by iron and fire. Not eight or eighty, you are either zero or eight billion! Situations and feelings are either absolutely experienced and felt or completely abandoned—which often lead you to the edge of insanity. In the same way, your attitudes and your words, even unintentionally, flirt with violence and domination, which can drive people away and reinforce your feeling of loneliness, even in a crowd.

Helpful and always ready to face the biggest challenges—and, for you, the bigger the better—you often border on smugness because you believe you can accomplish anything without bearing the natural consequences of your choices. Still, you don't know the meaning of the word *fear* and are always willing to help those who ask for help, even if charity is not among your best abilities.

Intransigence and rebellion guide your steps, but does the world really live at war as it seems to you? Seeking balance is your destiny's greatest challenge—and the greatest difficulty you'll encounter along the way. For this you must first face your fears and accept that your will won't always prevail—in your case, this is exactly what will save you from yourself!

Alafia

Number: 16
Motto: At peace with the world and with you
Vibration: Female
Element of Nature: Air/Fire
Behavior: Patient/Impatient

Key Expressions

Positive	Negative
Pacifist	Fanciful and utopian
Curious and searching	Has difficulty making decisions
Enjoys volunteering and helping	Lives in affliction
Sympathetic character	Fears losing everything and everyone
Great humanitarian sense	

Curious and seeking by nature, you follow in the footsteps of peace to find the great victories of destiny. The generosity and understanding of human beings are your greatest qualities, and it is through them that you evolve materially and spiritually.

Always dedicated to helping others, no matter how heavy the burden, you recognize the efforts and struggles necessary for practical goals to be realized. With this, you're aware that peace cannot be achieved without fighting wars, and you also know the strategies for achieving it. However, even though you know all this, you avoid any kind of clash, preferring dialogue and mediation to conflict.

All of this, however, pushes you beyond the limit of optimism, flirting with fantasy and being naive about real human nature. When forced to see it, you suffer from the shock of reality against your well-designed idealism.

You create expectations about the goodness of people and situations around you, but it is precisely this utopia that makes you lose yourself in the ways of the world. By the way, have you ever thought about what you truly need to do to have peace? Meditating about it will make you find answers that you never imagined and that will be extremely important to alleviate the chaos that insists on haunting your soul.

The constant affliction that plagues your heart is mainly due to your difficulty in making choices. The universe opens in front of you, and having to decide to follow a path and give up other options tortures your soul. In addition, your eternal fear of loss—of people, opportunities, and yourself—often ends up preventing you from leaving the dream world and taking your plans and goals off the paper. Precisely for this reason, it is necessary to learn that every dream can be fulfilled, but it is necessary to maintain a sense of reality even when your heart drives you to defend the most difficult causes.

With your eyes on the future, you have a beautiful path to develop in your life—always forward, optimistic, and positive. By finding the balance of the real and the imaginary, you will be able to accomplish great things for yourself and for those around you, building a legacy that will surely last for generations.

◗ A Deeper Look

Based on the information that you have learned about the birth Odu, what is the behavioral style of your Odu Ori?

( ) Dominant

( ) Extroverted

( ) Analytical

( ) Patient

Is the behavioral style you pointed out earlier, based on how you see yourself at this point in life, the same as your Odu Ori defines?

( ) Yes, it's the same!   ( ) No, they're different.

If yes, what other behavioral styles can you perceive in yourself? And which characteristics of it are most present in your life today?

( ) Dominant

( ) Extroverted

( ) Analytical

( ) Patient

_____

_____

_____

If no, what characteristics in yourself made you choose the first behavior?

_____

_____

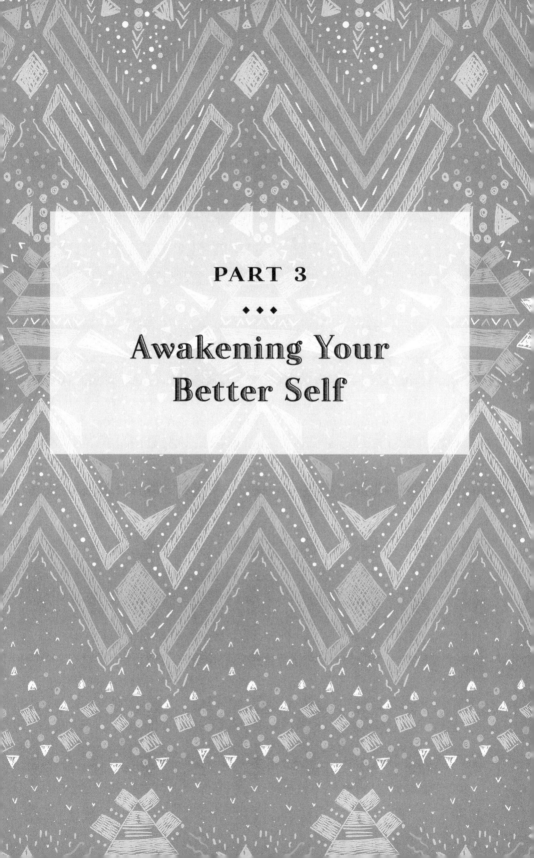

PART 3

•••

Awakening Your Better Self

8

Transforming Others through Self-Transformation

How often, no matter how sincerely and profoundly you look at yourself and the influences that the birth Odus and the outer world have on you, does it seem almost impossible to take responsibility for what happens? How many times—no matter how sincere and profound your work of inner revolution—do you feel that the people around you, and especially those with whom you are most intimate, are not in the same rhythm and do not realize that the conflicts among all of you could be avoided with small changes in attitude? How many times have you wished you were able to transform whoever is beside you, as if the other person's change in behavior could make your own change become even more true and powerful?

Believe me: this is possible! But I need to be honest with you: none of us are perfect, and above all, every change starts within us and only then expands. Therefore, no one changes the other without first changing him- or herself! Come with me, I'll show you how.

The main and biggest problem in these situations is that noticing the other person's mistakes is always much easier. Our physical eyes see the outside and can quickly identify every little slip and every little quality. Our moral scale receives this information and, in an instant, creates opinions about what the eyes have seen. We then refer to our own experiences of life, our achievements and frustrations, and promptly issue the verdict on what, in the other person, could be changed so that he or she could achieve success and happiness.

However, all this agility and ability to indicate the changes to make and paths to follow to achieve happiness does not work with the same speed when, instead of looking outside with our physical eyes, we seek to look inside with the eyes of the soul. *Your opinions* are created and based on *your experiences, mistakes, and successes* to ensure that you reach *your goals*. But who said that the other—whom your physical eyes saw and your moral scale opined about—wants the same things that you do? Who says that the flaws and mistakes you see in another are viewed negatively by them? Who says that another person sees what you see in them? And who says, above all, that the other person *wants to change* this or that aspect of his or her life?

In the same way, who is the one that is seeking to change? Who finally decides to recognize and enhance the greatest qualities and, at the same time, unravel and neutralize the negative characteristics in a personality? Who, in this present day, decides to begin this transformation?

But I said that it is possible to change others, and I reaffirm that this is true! First, though, I want to tell you a story that will put things into perspective.

PLATO'S CAVE

Plato was an ancient Greek philosopher and mathematician who lived between 428 BCE and 348 BCE. He was the author of several philosophy studies and founder of the Academy in Athens, the first institution of higher education in the Western world. Considered one of the central figures in the history of philosophy, Plato also helped to structure philosophy, science, and spirituality as we know them today.

Among many of his most famous writings is the Myth of the Cave, or the Allegory of the Cave, a metaphor about the human condition facing the real world, which teaches us about the importance of knowledge and personal enlightenment over ignorance. And what is the work

of unraveling the birth Odus and inner revolution if not a quest to illuminate the depths of our soul?

According to the Myth of the Cave, which is in Book 7 of Plato's
Republic, the process of awakening consciousness goes through two
stages: the mastery of sensory things and the mastery of ideas. In Plato's
analysis, reality is in the world of ideas, of what we think and how we
perceive the world, and most of humanity lives in ignorance—in the
world of sensible things—of what we receive from outside and consume
without questioning and, which are mutable and subject to mostly
unknown interpretations and contexts. The original text of the myth
is a dialogue between Socrates, who was Plato's mentor, and his two
brothers, Glaucus and Adimantus. In the following excerpt, I transcribe
only Socrates's speeches, which illustrate the myth.

Imagine men in an underground dwelling, in the form of a cave,
with an entrance open to light; these men have been there since
childhood, with legs and necks in chains, so that they cannot move
or see anything but what is in front of them, for the chains prevent them from turning their heads; light comes to them from a fire
burning on a hill that rises behind them; between the fire and the
prisoners passes an ascending road. Imagine that a small wall is built
along this road, like the partitions that puppeteers erect in front of
them and above which they display their wonders.

Imagine now, along this small wall, men carrying objects of all
kinds, that transpose them: figurines of men and animals, of stone,
wood and all kinds of matter. Naturally, among these transporters,
some speak, and others follow in silence.

They resemble us. And, to begin with, do you think that, in
such a condition, they have ever seen, of themselves and their companions, more than the shadows cast by the fire on the wall of
the cave opposite them? So, if they could communicate with each
other, don't you think they would mistake the shadows they see
for real objects?

What if the back wall of the prison echoed whenever one of the transporters spoke, wouldn't they think they heard the shadow that passed in front of them? In this way, will such men only attribute reality to the shadows of manufactured objects?

Consider now what will happen to them, of course, if they are released from their chains and cured of their ignorance. Let one of these prisoners be freed, let him be forced to straighten up immediately, turn his neck, walk, raise his eyes to the light: in making all these movements he will suffer . . . how do you think he will respond if anyone comes to tell him that until then he had seen nothing but ghosts—and that now, closer to reality and real objects, he sees more accurately? Will the shadows he saw in the past seem truer to him than the objects they show him now?

And if they yank him out of his cave, force him up the rough and steep slope, and don't let go of him before they've dragged him into the sunlight, won't he suffer heartily and complain of such violence? He will start by distinguishing the shadows more easily; then, the images of men and objects reflected in the waters; finally, the objects themselves. After that, facing the brightness of the stars and the Moon, he will be able to contemplate, during the night, the celestial bodies and the sky itself more easily than, during the day, the Sun and its light. . . .

Now, remembering his first abode, the wisdom that is professed there and those who were his companions in captivity, do you not think that he will rejoice in the move and regret those who remained there?

Or, like the hero of Homer, would he not prefer a thousand times to be a simple farmer, and suffer everything in the world, than to return to the old illusions and live as he used to?

Imagine that this man returns to the cave and goes to sit in his old place: will he not be blinded by the darkness as he abruptly leaves the sunlight?

And if he has to enter again into competition with the prisoners who have not freed themselves from their chains, to judge these shadows, while his vision is still confused and before his eyes have recovered, because getting used to the darkness will take quite a while in the long run, won't he make others laugh at his expense and say that, having gone up there, he'd come back with spoiled eyes, so it's not worth trying to go up there? And if someone tries to free and lead upward, would that someone not kill him if he could do it?

An animated version of this myth can be seen on YouTube, narrated in Portuguese by Rodrigo Freire. This version summarizes the original story and clearly shows, in my opinion, how raising awareness and doing the work of inner revolution can be fundamental to understanding how it is possible to change others by understanding our own birth Odus. What follows is a translation of Rodrigo's version of the myth.

Imagine prisoners who spend their entire lives tied up in a cave. They've been tied up so they can't look behind them; they can only look at the wall in front of them.

At their back is a fire and between them and the fire is a path. Imagine that every day a variety of objects pass along the path, and, of course, the people who lead their lives and their shapes create mysterious shadows on the wall. This is the only world the prisoners have ever known: the shadows of objects they have never seen.

Now imagine that one of the prisoners is released. After taking some time to adapt to the strong light, the freed prisoner begins to experience the world for the first time, and it doesn't look like anything he could have imagined.

With his new perception of the world, the man evidently wants to go back and share his amazing discoveries with his old friends. But the other prisoners cannot recognize their own friend! He looks like all things: his voice is a distorted echo and his body, a grotesque shadow. They cannot understand his fantastic story about the world outside the cave. For them, this world does not exist. *But that doesn't make the world outside the cave any less real.*

There are two lessons in the Myth of the Cave that we need to examine carefully and that apply directly to the inner revolution and how the study of birth Odus can transform others from within ourselves. The first and perhaps most important lesson is to understand that life *before* unraveling your Odus is like the life of the prisoners in the cave: none of them is wrong or can be condemned for believing the shadows are real and are terrifying threats. They are, in fact, dangerous and threatening *from the perspective of the prisoners,* who have never seen beyond the shadows and do not know that the objects passing behind the wall exist. In the same way, when we live life without understanding *how and why we act and react to the reality around us* we are like those prisoners in the cave. So, just as it is impossible to expect prisoners to stop fearing the shadows and believe that they are mere projections on the wall without first experiencing reality in the light, it is also not possible to simply expect the people we live with, work with, and love can believe that they are capable of transforming the negative aspects of their personalities without first seeing it happen with their own eyes.

The second lesson is that even if you break free from the chains of ignorance and experience life outside the cave—that is, however much you understand your birth Odus and experience true transformation— the most you can do in relation to others is to *tell about what you lived,* running the risk that, as the original version of the story says, "the others would laugh at your expense and say that, having gone up there, you came back with spoiled eyesight." That is why it is critical, once you are freed from these chains, that you make a personal commitment to yourself and those you love to *tell them what the world is like out here.* When you have truly transformed, you will realize that the risk of their laughter at your expense is worth taking. Still, you need to keep in mind that this effort is only worthwhile when those who listen to you also want to free themselves and that, therefore, your mission in life is not to save everyone!

As a matter of fact, it is necessary to clarify that the change will not be of the other per se but of the ways in which, for each aspect of the Orisha birth chart, it is possible to *model our personal characteristics to the characteristics of the other.* From this modeling, it will then be possible to adapt your actions, impressions, and external reactions to theirs, and finally, the result of this interaction—without you losing or giving up your identity—is to achieve the desired change or, rather, the desired response of the other. For this to be possible, however, it is necessary to remember what we have learned about the positive and negative aspects of each Odu, as well as the areas of life governed by the major and minor houses—both in yours and in the Orisha birth chart of the person who you want to transform. I'll give you a real example, based on my personal birth Odu.

As I mentioned before, the main rulership of my birth (Odu Ori) is defined by Odu Iorossun—the path of language, rationality, and communication. This same Odu is also my regent in Apá Òtún, the intellectual and professional paths of my life. Imagine, now, that I have a very important business meeting in which I will sign a professional contract, and I know in advance that the person I will have this meeting with is governed by Odu Ejilaxebora in the Odu Ori position (the main house that governs his identity) or Oju Ori (the major house that defines his temperament). With this information and the interpretation of this Odu, magic can happen.

Although it is impossible for me to force him to agree with everything I will say at the meeting and accept all conditions or proposals, from the assessment of his regency I know that he is a bureaucratic person, linked to numbers and results, and that he likes to be exalted and validated as a king. In the same way, I know that one of my greatest qualities is the analysis of information and mathematical data, logical and analytical reasoning, and my tendency, as a "conciliator father," to seek the balance point where all parties involved in the situation feel they are winning together. Therefore, it is up to me to prepare the meeting script, graphs, and reports, as well as the way to communicate this information so that, while keeping a commitment to the *truth of the facts,* the other person will realize that, in one way or another, he will also be getting advantages and achievements by accepting what I propose.

Another example, still about my personal regency: I have Odu Iorossun in the main house (Odu Ori) and Odu Ejiogbe in Apá Osi, the Odu of personal relationships. Evaluating only the negative aspects of these two Odus and without considering any prior effort on my inner transformation, it is possible to identify that (1) I am jealous and possessive of what I like and love and (2) I have a dominant personality, with a tendency to establish rules and limits. Now imagine that I begin a love relationship with a person who is ruled by the Odu Obara in Odu Ori and by the Odu Eta-Ogunda in Apá Osi. Well, if I don't consciously work on the negative aspects of my birth Odus, this will be a relationship of constant conflicts; after all, both Obara and Eta-Ogunda are Odus that deal with freedom, with not letting oneself be commanded, and with difficulty in following established rules!

Can I force the person to follow rules and standards? No, I can't. But can I balance the way I *communicate* my wishes and desires, or even how I show affection without smothering his freedom? Absolutely, yes!

At the same time, his Odu Obara in Odu Ori indicates the tendency to extroversion, and an ease of making friends, but also the need for attention and care due to the ingenuity that this Odu imprints on its rulers. In the same way, my Odu Iorossun in Odu Ori gives me a paternal, sustaining character who assumes practical responsibilities so that the other can dream without getting lost along the way. In this analysis—taking care that I do not assume the role of *father* in this relationship; after all, we are dealing with a love relationship—I can equalize my personal characteristics with those of my partner so that his joviality, defined by Odu Obara, is balanced by my maturity, given to me by Odu Iorossun.

These are two real examples of how, even if we are not able to change the other directly, we can adapt the influences of our personal birth Odus to other people's birth Odus and influence the outcome of situations. In an allusion to the Myth of the Cave, even when it is not possible to free other prisoners (even because some of them *do not want to be freed*), it is still possible to either tell them about how we live or, ultimately and without their knowledge, project in the shadows the shapes we desire. For this to happen in the most effective way, of course, we need to know the birth Odus of the person we will be interacting with, and when it comes to love relationships, we need to look at the combination of birth Odus that will result in the love and relationship Odus assessment, which we will see in chapter 9.

However, just as it is important to understand and interpret the Myth of the Cave and how the lessons learned therein can guide us in shaping our reality, it is also important for us to know another myth.

SISYPHUS'S STONE

In Greek mythology, Sisyphus was the son of King Aeolus and was considered the most cunning of all mortals, a master of malice and happiness, and is still known as one of the greatest offenders of the gods. He was the founder and first king of Ephira, later called Corinth, where he ruled for several years. The following is a translation of the myth as presented in the book *O Poder da Autorresponsabilidade* (The Power of Self-Responsibility) by Paulo Vieira (2017).

> One of the most interesting characters in Greek mythology is Sisyphus, the king of Corinth. He was thought to be the smartest among men. Despite all his cunning, or perhaps precisely because of it, he was always faced with the most complicated situations. Each cleverness created new difficulties, which in turn called for new stratagems, in a succession of temporary solutions.
>
> Once, Sisyphus discovered by chance that Zeus had kidnapped Aegina, daughter of Asop, the god of rivers. As there was a lack of water in his lands, Sisyphus had the idea of revealing to Asop the whereabouts of his daughter, if he gave him a spring in return. The desperate father gladly accepted the proposal. He gave Sisyphus the spring and then learned that his daughter had been kidnapped by Zeus.
>
> Sisyphus had water, but he ran into another problem: Zeus was

furious with the denunciation and sent Death to fetch him.

Trusting in his own cunning, Sisyphus received Death and began to talk. He praised her beauty and asked her to let her neck be adorned with a necklace. The necklace, in fact, was nothing more than a collar, with which Sisyphus kept Death imprisoned and managed to circumvent its fate.

For a while, no one else died. Sisyphus knew how to deceive Death, but he got into new trouble. This time with Pluto, the god of souls and the unconscious, and with Mars, the god of war, who needed the services of Death to consummate the battles. As soon as he hear about what had happened, Pluto freed Death and ordered him to bring Sisyphus immediately to hell. When Sisyphus said goodbye to his wife, he was careful to secretly ask her not to bury his body.

Already in hell, Sisyphus complained to Pluto of his wife's lack of respect in not burying her body. Then he pleaded for a day's deadline to get revenge on the ungrateful woman and fulfill the funeral rites. Pluto granted him the request. Sisyphus then took back his body and fled with his wife. He had deceived Death for the second time.

He lived in hiding for many years until he finally died. When Pluto saw him, he reserved a special punishment for him. He was ordered to push a huge boulder to the top of a mountain. Before reaching the top, however, the stone rolled down the mountain, forcing Sisyphus to resume his task until the end of time.

Interpreting the myth in the context of the birth Odus, we realize that it tells us about the human tendency to resist responsibility for one's own actions, living in an eternal restart and blaming others for what happens to them. Certain of his cleverness, Sisyphus spends eternity suffering from the same common problem, but he does not accept that he was the one who condemned himself: he points out and blames the origin of his suffering to the gods and to fate, which are immutable and over which he has no control.

◑ *What Are We Missing?*

Right now, what are the rocks you've been pushing uphill repeatedly throughout your life, only to see them roll down and take you back to where you started?

_____

_____

_____

_____

_____

_____

_____

THE CAVE, THE STONE, AND THE REAL WORLD

This reflection reminds me, however, not of a myth, but of a real story: the same one I told at the beginning of this book, about the woman who came looking for me to consult the cowrie shell divination and who, years later, continued to face the same problem over and over again. Here, then, are the two greatest lessons that Sisyphus teaches us: (1) the importance of recognizing the weight of your lifelong choices, as discussed in detail before; and (2) the urgency to realize that, in one way or another, we are all Sisyphus at some point in our lives.

These two lessons make even more sense when we think about how evaluating our birth Odus in combination with other people's birth Odus can result in shaping the results—and, why not say, shaping our future. In the myth, Sisyphus is condemned to carry *alone* the weight of the choices he made in his life; in the same way, just as we can consciously choose our present and our future, determining whether we will carry stones or feathers, it is our responsibility to make choices about life itself.

When comparing the myth of Sisyphus with the Myth of the Cave, we once again conclude that our limit is to present the light to the prisoners and to help those who are supposed to be cunning to reflect; we are not, however, responsible for breaking their shackles or carrying their stones. The work of interpreting your birth Odus and, especially, of achieving your inner revolution is a personal journey of rebirth of consciousness and of evolution; it's not an evangelizing mission. There will be those like you who will seek transformation; and there will also be those who will choose to carry their stones eternally, never realizing that they are the ones who choose to do so. Better to leave them to their burdens than to insist on opening their eyes to what they do not want to see.

9

The Inner Revolution

If you made it this far, believe me, you can already consider yourself victorious. Really! Although a large part of the book is theoretical teachings on how to calculate the birth Odus and interpret their meanings, I am sure that while you read, many questions and doubts about how you have been living and about how you have assumed the responsibilities for your destiny arose. And all true transformation begins, precisely, when we begin to question and meditate on who we are and who we want to become. However, I must confess one thing: everything we've seen so far is just a timid first step on the journey of self-knowledge and personal discovery you are about to take—and it is from now on that change begins!

Apart from the myths of Ifá, the cave, and Sisyphus, all the stories I've told so far are real and were lived by me or by the people around me, and the one I'm going to tell you now is no different. It is real and will completely change the way you look at the negative aspects of birth Odus and the challenges of fate.

One of the most common mistakes I see people making is thinking that an Orisha priest has no problems or that he solves his problems like magic. I wish it were like that! I'm as human as you are and also face life's provocations like everyone else, but through the guidance of the Orishas, I'm also learning how to overcome them every day.

The truth is that life is not easy. The world has more and more people every day, and life seems to pass faster than ever. We are more than seven billion people, each one with his or her different desires and personalities, trying to survive the chaos of the modern world. But as my grandmother used to say, *dripping water hollows out stone.*

It may sound cruel to say this, but I know you'll understand: none of these seven billion people are 100 percent good all the time. Like everything else in the universe, each of us carries hidden fears, desires, and frightening fantasies. Even today, thousands of years after Plato, it seems that the caves of life continue to imprison us, and we go on forever in fear of our own shadows.

As in the Myth of the Cave, most people I know who have achieved some degree of personal or spiritual evolution say the same thing: at some point in their journey, when they left the safe path of the known, they had to face their greatest fears and their worst flaws to reach enlightenment. And I must confess: my shadows have already made me a very difficult person to deal with. Sagittarius, initiated to Oshossi and ruled by Odu Iorossun—imagine that! It was only when I started to consciously recognize and work over my shadows that I became able to transform (or, rather, transmute) my life and experience more peace, success, and happiness.

The first time I saw this happening, I almost couldn't believe it. By this time, I had already studied my Orisha birth chart and started to understand how my birth Odus define and influence my personality in a positive and negative way. However, it was only when I accepted knowing myself more deeply and looking with attention and courage to the most negative aspects of each one of them that I learned, then, to anticipate their omens and transform each difficulty into opportunity, each defect into potential.

At this point, maybe you're trying to figure out what your shadow is. Maybe you've even identified a part of it while reading the book and learning about your personal Odus, but don't know to deal with it. Or maybe you're already working on some of these aspects. But believe what I'm going to say now: if you don't delve deeply into the darker aspects of your personality and aren't willing to face them head on, no change will be real, and the victories in your life certainly won't last.

As we talked about in the first chapters of this book, everyone knows that we live in a world of energies that complete and complement one another through opposition and vibrational balance. However, as is natural to all human beings, we are guided to seek and therefore look only on the positive side of these energies, living in a utopia of absolute goodness. Well, we are human and, therefore, flawed. We are evolving; we haven't reached enlightenment yet. So, no matter what our faith is, no matter where or how you practice spirituality, you and I will always be subject to the influence of our shadows and sometimes the shadows of others.

What most people don't understand is that there is beauty in darkness and teaching in the shadows! And what is, after all, the shadow in the Orisha birth chart? We have already seen that all Odus have their positive and negative aspects, which influence us in each of the major and minor houses on the map. But one of them, Osogbo Ori, always presents itself in its negative vibration and has the power to negate all other Odus in our maps. It is from there that our journey toward facing the shadows begins.

If you are satisfied with the basic interpretations of your Orisha birth chart so far and believe that you are not ready to take a new step toward your personal enlightenment, that is fine, I understand. But if you are really determined and committed to awakening your best self and deeply transforming your life and destiny going forward, then you need to look inside yourself and prepare to unravel the greatest mysteries of your *inner world,* acknowledging all aspects of your regency, including and especially those that can detract from your paths.

That's why many people suffer the same situations over and over throughout their lives and give up on knowing themselves: they do all the possible rituals and make offerings to attract positivity, but they do not seek to understand the deviations and setbacks on their path, which prevent these blessings from reaching them. In short, the universe is an inexhaustible source of victories, and the Orishas bless each of us in infinite ways, but for this to reach us, we need to be willing to walk the path given by them and be prepared to receive their teachings.

If you sincerely understand the statements *I am responsible for all the good and evil that comes my way; I deserve the good and accept and receive it; I recognize the evil, face it, and transform it,* then you will have already taken a big step forward. I say this because I have already lived it through my skin, and I will tell you a little more about this experience.

HOW HAVE THE SHADOWS AFFECTED ME?

As you already know, each of us carries within us the regency of the six Odus in the major houses of our map:

* One main Odu, called Odu Ori, is always positive.
* Four secondary ones govern different areas of our life.
* Osogbo Ori is always negative and is responsible for the challenges of destiny.

In my case, in Odu Ori, I am governed by Odu Iorossun, the Odu of intellect, intelligence, and analytical thinking. His rulers tend to think a lot all the time, to plan everything in detail before deciding, to anticipate all the possibilities and the what-ifs of every step they take in life. That would be great if it weren't for the other aspects of this Odu, which often make me think so much and have so many ideas at the same time and want to plan everything in such detail so that things are perfect that I end up stalling.

Along with this, in Osogbo Ori, I carry Odu Odi, the path of the most serious challenges, the provocations of fate, distrust, and dangers. To top it off, in addition to all the features that commonly come along with Odu Odi, which by far are not the best that could be, whoever has this regency in Osogbo Ori repeatedly sees their plans and projects die on the vine! And that was exactly how things happened to me: constantly I found myself one step closer to conquering what I had been looking for, and at the last minute something simple appeared that made everything go down the drain, and I had to start again, practically from scratch. That's why those who have Odu Odi in their birth Odus have as a motto in life: persist where anyone else would give up!

HOW THE TRANSFORMATION HAPPENED

Just between us, it is obvious and natural that we always look first for what is good for us, for what is beautiful, and, above all, for what agrees with us. Therefore, when I started to unveil my birth Odus, I plunged headlong into each of the positive points of these regency, focusing my attention, my purpose, and my attitudes to enhance each one of them. It was so amazing to see how they described me, how the interpretation of each house on the map seemed to take a picture of my whole life.

I didn't care about the negatives. I noticed, of course, some aspects of them that made sense. But, as you probably are right now, I didn't recognize that, just as the positives described me and made me feel like the most special guy in the world, the negative aspects of my birth Odus showed in detail each of my worst flaws and, in a way, explained many of the pains I had experienced so far.

It wasn't easy, but at a certain point I was forced to accept that all those aspects also described me and that I wasn't as good, complete, and perfect as I wanted to believe. At many key points in my life, I was, in fact, a prisoner in the cave, chained, blind, and terrified of the shadows in front of me and especially the shadows inside me. I slowly began to realize that those shadows were a fundamental part of my personality. In each of the positive points, I was actually as excellent as I imagined myself to be. On the other hand, in each of the negative aspects, I was just as deficient and harmful to myself as I refused to admit.

It was time to change that—and that's when the magic started to happen.

When I admitted to myself that I was the sum of both aspects, light and shadow, and came to recognize that the negative aspect of my birth Odus also affected and ruled the way I had been living so far, I dedicated myself to learning how I could avoid them. But the *true transformation* happened when I consciously decided to look at my Osogbo Ori regency—that's what *turned the key* in my life!

Instead of lying to myself, saying over and over that the chains that held me inside the cave were unbreakable or that the stories heard from the outside were pure invention, for a moment I looked at those chains, recognized their existence, and realized that the key to free myself from them was also there. Already freed, but still adjusting my gaze from the cold darkness of the cave to the new world that presented itself with a little light, I could then see that the shadows . . . Ah! The shadows that had terrified me for so long were just that: inanimate projections, incapable of attacking or harming me. They only had the strength that I gave them.

Well, since the first years of my life, Odu Iorossun gave me the ability to foresee all the possibilities, to plan with peace of mind each step to take to conquer my desires, and to seek excellence in everything I did. But Odu Odi insisted on making me distrust everything and everyone, reinforcing the anguish and apprehension about what could go wrong, training my eyes to see only the negative side of each situation, catching me by surprise at the last minute with obvious unforeseen circumstances, and often tempting me to give up after trying so hard. What would happen, then, if I recognized in advance Odi's threats on the way ahead and applied Iorossun's potentials on them?

It was my work on each of the negative aspects of my birth Odus and especially the meditations on Osogbo Ori's characteristics that led me to victory. Recognizing its shadows, I consciously chose to be the light on my own path. From there, I finally began to train myself to stop looking into a future that never came, repeatedly carrying Odi's stones up the mountain, and started to look at what was happening now, in the present, and how each step taken here could profoundly transform what I would find ahead.

YOU CAN TAKE THE FIRST STEP, TOO

I told you all this because, like me, I'm sure you've been living through several situations that seem to have no solution and are endlessly repeated. And the truth is that you may already know your qualities, do the best you can all the time, and value each of your achievements. But if you don't recognize your flaws right now and decide to face the shadows of your personality and consciously work on them, nothing will change! At the same time, I'm also sure that you have incredible positive potential, extraordinary qualities that can be used to *turn the key* in your life, as I did in mine.

I'm not going to teach you a magic formula for making this happen. This formula, to be honest, doesn't exist! But I can tell you, having lived through all of this and having been exactly where you are today, that the key to this transformation is within you, even if you don't see it right now. Our journey in this book is almost over, but before we say our good-byes, I want to invite you to take one last step so that you, too, can leave the cave.

◖ Our Personal Odus, Light and Shadow

The negative of my birth (Osogbo Ori) is:

_____

These are the three main shadows this Odu casts on my life:

_____

_____

_____

The positive of my birth (Odu Ori) is:

_____

These are the six main lights this Odu projects into my life:

_____

_____

_____

_____

_____

_____

At this point in my life, and just for today, I realize that the shadows of Osogbo Ori affect me in the following way:

_____

_____

_____

_____

_____

_____

But I recognize that for today and forever, the light of Odu Ori will be able to overcome these shadows. For this, I commit myself to:

_____

_____

_____

_____

_____

_____

_____

_____

Starting today, every day when you wake up, look at yourself in the mirror and read aloud what you wrote.

Each morning, when you finish the first reading, read aloud only the last answer twice more, take a deep breath, and notice how the shadows will give way to the light inside you!

10

Other Applications
of African Numerology

The most important tools of African numerology are, without a doubt, identifying the birth Odus, interpreting them, and, above all, doing personal work on the inner revolution. Still, other techniques can also be applied based on numerology's assessments and lessons, and that's what I will teach you about now. All these other applications, however, are based on what we have learned so far. Therefore, to make the best use of them, it is important that you thoroughly master the meanings and interpretations of the birth Odus and their combinations.

PERSONAL YEAR ODUS

Knowing yourself is a big decision on the journey of personal growth and evolution, and you've already taken the first step in unraveling your birth Odus. Now, how about continuing that journey and discovering your personal year's predictions and Odus?

Just as the birth Odus govern your decisions and choices from the inner world, through African numerology it is also possible to identify some trends and influences of the regent Odus of the month and the year your living, as energies coming from the outer world to your destiny. And, as we learned together, from the moment you anticipate the events of the future, you can consciously act on your choices in the present with greater certainty.

Thinking this way, this is undoubtedly the biggest mistake that most people who come to consult the cowrie shell divination with me make: they seek guidance and help from the Orishas after the problems are already happening. They forget the old saying that it's better to be safe than sorry!

The truth is that when we know the spiritual rulers that will be guiding us from now on, everything becomes easier. All the people I know who are really in tune with their personal transformation seek to learn from the past, act in the present, and prepare for the future—whether through analysis and financial planning, through New Year's resolutions, or even through the reading of oracles and predictions.

I'll even reveal a secret to you: I've suffered a lot, frustrating myself when I saw my plans go wrong by simply doing what I wanted, when I wanted, and the way I wanted—until I started to trust my decisions to the Orishas. Nowadays, I don't make any important decision in my life without first consulting Eshu and the cowrie shell divination to find out if it's the right time to take this or that step in my life.

I don't know about you, but I'm always looking forward to two special moments of the year: New Year's Eve and my birthday, when my personal year's regency changes—and that's my favorite date! It's in these two moments that I renew my hopes, review the lessons learned from what I've been through in recent months, balance mistakes and successes, and outline new goals for the following year. Before that, however, I always observe the Odus that will be influencing each month of my life from then on and the predictions they have for me, besides, of course, finding out who the new year's regent Orisha will be and doing my rituals to attract these positive energies into my life.

What almost no one knows—and those who know usually don't tell—is that, far beyond oracle predictions, what really influences our lives and our destiny are the Odus who will be ruling the months of the year we live, which are defined from our date of birth and not the Gregorian or civil calendar, and the way they combine with our birth Odus.

Each of us has different energies, which receive the vibrations of our birth Odus, the Orisha of the year, and the Odus related to the running of our personal month and year. More than that, each month of our life has different rulers, which are defined by three factors:

- The birth Odus, which accompany you from the beginning to the end of life
- The Orishas and the Odus ruling the civil year in which we live
- The regent Odus of your personal year, which changes every year on our birthday

That's why sometimes predictions seem generic, and many of them just don't happen in our lives. From the moment you understand that each person is a unique divine particle and treads a unique path in life and seeks to connect with the path that differentiates your destiny from others, you will have taken a big step toward happiness and the true transformation of your life.

Identifying the regent Odu of your personal year is simple, and the calculation should be done by adding each digit of your date of birth and changing the *year of your birth* to the *year of your last birthday,* following the same reduction rules you have already learned. For example, imagine that today is June 22, 2020, and we are going to calculate the personal year Odu for the birth date of September 21, 1958. As the person has not yet had a birthday this year, we do the math based on his or her past year:

$$2 + 1 + 0 + 9 + 2 + 0 + 1 + 9 = \mathbf{24} = 2 + 4 = \mathbf{6}$$

Regent Odu from September 21, 2019, until September 20, 2020: **Obara**

Now, imagine that today is October 22, 2020, and therefore, the person in the example has already had a birthday this year, so we'll use 2020 in the personal year calculation, so:

$$2 + 1 + 0 + 9 + 2 + 0 + 2 + 0 = \mathbf{16}$$

Regent Odu from September 21, 2020, to September 20, 2021: **Alafia**

The personal year Odu is an influence from the outer world, which changes each time you have a birthday and rules you for the next twelve months. See how easy it is? To interpret it, just follow the same system and pattern you learned for your Orisha birth chart.

LOVE AND RELATIONSHIP ODUS

Take a deep breath, relax, and now answer sincerely:

* If you knew the paths and challenges of your dating or marriage . . .
* If you knew the ways to prevent and correct mistakes before they happen between you both . . .
* If you could guarantee a more affectionate and harmonious relationship with your partner, discovering how to deal with difficult moments in your relationship . . .

What would your life be like? Does it seem like fantasy?
Trust me when I tell you: this is possible!

During our journey, we learned what the Odus are, how they serve as a pathway for communication between humans and the Orishas and how they relate to all areas of our life and influence our personality and the choices that we make.

As we have also seen, the Odus are related and intertwined with everything that happens to us, to other people, and to situations around us. Therefore, when we decide to change the path taken or start a new project in our lives, new energies are formed and begin to influence and modify one another.

It also happens when you decide it's time to leave your parents' home and share a new house with friends, for example. Or when you decide to start a partnership or a new business. Or when you decide to be with someone, date, or get married.

We all dress according to the people we live with; we speak the same slang and expressions; we go to the same places, and sometimes we even act and feel like them. And believe me, they also dress, talk, act, and feel similar and are influenced by you! Human coexistence is essential for our spiritual and material evolution, and it is impossible to remain detached from it. However, getting along doesn't always mean living in peace. People are complex and have different backgrounds, cultures, moods, and histories, which make them who they are and make them act and react the way they do.

How many dating relationships and marriages that had everything going for them have you seen come to an end because of communication failures between the two people or simply because the way that one partner communicates his or her love is different and opposite to the way the other expects to receive it?

How many friendships have ceased to exist because one friend wanted and expected to be treated with patience and gentleness and the other friend expressed himself in a more direct and objective manner?

How many companies and businesses, even very profitable ones, have gone bankrupt because the way one partner managed and led was incompatible with the methods of the other?

How many abandoned loves and separated families? How many lost friendships? How many companies gone out of business and employees laid off?

Self-Knowledge Is the First Step

Every meeting between two people is a relationship, whether of lovers, friends, family members, or colleagues. And every meeting is subject to the differences between its parts. Therefore, getting to know ourselves and the people around us, understanding their desires and fears and the correct ways to act with each one of them, is fundamental for harmonious coexistence.

In addition to identifying and understanding the birth Odus through African numerology, it is also possible to identify the energies that govern these encounters and understand in detail how one person will affect another, what the positive and negative aspects are to be worked out between them, and how it is possible to correct mistakes and reconcile conflicts in a relationship even before they happen.

Before learning how to do this, let's quickly recap the concepts learned about the Orisha birth chart and about which Odus define your personality, your paths, and the challenges that fate has for you:

- **Odu Ori** defines identity.
- **Oju Ori** governs temperament and intellect.
- **Ikoko Ori** determines personal evolution.
- **Apá Òtún** defines rational intellectual aspects.
- **Apá Osi** governs emotional and sentimental aspects.
- **Osogbo Ori** determines the challenges of destiny.

Now imagine that in a relationship there are at least two people involved, which means their personalities, energies, and personal rules need to combine and balance so that they can get along in the best way. Whether in a relationship with a lover, friend, coworker, or family member, each person we live or work with has his or her own qualities, personality traits, tastes, desires, and defects. In addition to those aspects—and especially when we think about love relationships—there are still other important issues that need to be considered for this union to work. For example, how many times have you met couples who work incredibly well alone, but everything changes when they're among friends?

Emotionally, each one of us has incorporated the family nucleus into which we were born and raised, the experiences we have had since childhood, the sum of the people with whom we currently interact, and the way we address each of these experiences, past and present. A person raised in a single-parent family will naturally experience a much greater influence from that one parent, and this influence will influence both his or her childhood and adolescence, as well as adulthood. When two people meet and decide to live by together, they need to identify and understand what emotional baggage each of them carries, what outside influences they have received, and how this has been interfering in their way of dealing with the world and the people around them. And they must try, even if little by little and with great delicacy, to establish limits so that the union is not compromised by factors that go beyond the two people involved. It's more or less like a mathematical calculation where the sum of $1 + 1$ gives more than 2.

For all these reasons and in order to understand these influences, characteristics, and rules of a couple's love combination, it is necessary, above all, to identify and analyze the set of birth Odus of each person involved, separately. Only after this initial analysis, which we learned in previous chapters, will we then be able to rightly combine both sets of energies and identify which new rulers are formed from this combination, understanding if and how this relationship can be beneficial to you and to the person by your side. After all, a good love must add to one's life and make each grow happily as a person!

From the combination and identification of the six birth Odus of each person involved, it will then be possible to define the six Odus that will determine the success and challenges of this relationship:

- **Odu Okolayà** (*relationship identity*): This Odu is the energy that defines the spiritual combination of the couple and the type of relationship they will have; after all, love, passion, friendship, and fellowship are completely different.
- **Odu Olóbirin** (*horizons and objectives*): Olóbirin determines how the couple develops their plans and objectives and the horizons they will reach side by side.

- **Odu Óna** (*relationship evolution*): This Odu is the energy that governs the evolution of the relationship, the transformations that the couple will experience over time, their growth as a couple, and the foreseen duration of the relationship.
- **Odu Ehin-Ode** (*external influences*): Ehin-Ode points out the public dynamics of the couple when they're in the outer world, as well as indicating which external influences will affect the stability of the relationship.
- **Odu Ídaiyafo** (*intimate life*): This is the Odu of sensuality and intimacy, which governs the way the couple will relate when at home alone and how their feelings develop as the relationship evolves.
- **Osogbo Ìfé** (*dangers and challenges to the couple*): Osogbo Ìfé presents the negative aspects of the relationship and influences all the regent love Odus. It determines the dangers and challenges to be overcome in the couple's search for a lasting relationship and what they need to focus attention on for their harmonious coexistence.

As with the birth Odus, identifying the relationship Odus and analyzing their influences enables a couple to prepare for the challenges that living together brings and to anticipate the challenges of destiny that lie ahead. With this, a couple can learn the positives that can be leveraged and avoid repeating patterns that make it difficult for them to show and receive love the way they both want, with more chances to live in harmony.

ODUS FOR BUSINESSES

Just like human beings, companies and businesses in general are also governed by their own energies—especially when we talk about companies, projects, or businesses that were founded by us. Much more than money and work, we put our dreams into a business. With that, in one way or another, a business or project also ends up gaining a life within our lives.

Though a legal entity does not have a proper birth date, it does have its foundation or inauguration date, and from that date we can apply the same techniques learned in the Orisha birth chart to understand each major house and minor house and their influences. For this, of course, we need to contextualize the regency:

How does this company, as a living entity, perceive itself, and how does it project its image and brand to the outer world?

How do the company's managers deal with the strategic planning for the business? In what ways is this planning put into practice?

How are the relationships with employees and between partners?

What challenges will the company face in its journey of existence and growth?

Finally, for each regent Odu of the business assessment, it will be possible to contextualize what we have learned about the Orisha birth chart of an individual.

The key point—and perhaps the biggest advantage—is that because a company, unlike a human being, does not have a birth date but a date that marks the beginning of its activities, its regency can be resignified. This means that, if we are analyzing the regent Odus of a new business that has not yet opened, we can create its business Odus assessment for several possible dates and compare the results of each one, choosing the best one for the official release of the new venture.

On the other hand, if the company already exists, and for some reason, we notice that its regency is negatively influencing the progress of the business, we can also prepare its assessment for some dates in the future and choose the best one to demarcate a reopening ceremony or the release of a new brand or advertising identity, for example. In this case, obviously, it will not be enough for this new date to denote just a party: just as on a personal level, it is necessary to face our shadows to carry out the inner revolution, an ongoing company that decides to modify its regency by choosing a new date will need to be prepared to, from then on, change its internal policy and effectively represent this transformation!

Another possibility that can be very significant, although quite laborious, is to apply the concepts learned about the birth Odus and the interpretation of the Orisha birth chart as a tool in choosing personnel. Whether for a new employee being hired, to promote an employee to a new position that requires a particular skill, or to develop relationship and interaction skills among members of a team, both the birth Odus and the combination of Odus of relationships can be an excellent tool to guide company choices (in the latter case, instead of interpreting the Odus in a love relationship context, obviously the focus should be on interpersonal and corporate relationships).

These same variations and contextualization can still be used in several other scenarios—family relationships, for example, can be analyzed through the Odus of love with a focus on fraternal relationships; the closing of a new commercial deal or the beginning of a professional partnership can be evaluated by combining the relationship Odus, reading through the environment for which it is intended.

There are countless possibilities for the application of African numerology and birth Odus in all areas of life and at any time. Therefore, it is important that every now and then you go back to reading your own regent Odus and try to understand how one or the other presents itself more intensely for this or that aspect of your life and how its positive and negative influences are repeated continuously without you realizing it—until you finally decide to wake up.

We are nearing the end of our journey, and by now you should have already calculated your birth Odus. Still, as a thank-you for your trust and company so far, I want to give you a gift: the full interpretation of the major houses on your map, written by me and especially for you!

To do this, just access the website www.diegodeoxossi.com.br /my-orishas-birth-chart and register using the promotional code **9786586174045.** You will receive by email the link to access the full version of your Orisha Birth Chart, free of charge!

Our journey ends now, but your transformation is just beginning.
Gratitude and abundance!

APPENDIX

Sample Worksheet Pages

HOW TO USE THIS SECTION

These worksheet pages will allow you to fill in your own Orisha birth chart. You should make copies of these pages so you can easily fill in multiple birth charts using the steps provided in the book. Then, for each chart, fill in the person's Odus and jot down key words from their descriptions that draw either that person's or your attention.

As a reminder, as we're working with sixteen distinct Odus, any number you get that is larger than sixteen will have both digits added together to find the appropriate Odu.

Odus

1. Okaran (see p. 100)
2. Ejioko (see p. 101)
3. Eta-Ogunda or Ogunda (see p. 103)
4. Iorossun (see p. 104)
5. Oshe (see p. 106)
6. Obara (see p. 108)
7. Odi (see p. 109)
8. Ejiogbe (see p. 111)
9. Ossa (see p. 113)
10. Ofun (see p. 115)
11. Owarin (see p. 117)
12. Ejilaxebora (see p. 118)
13. Ojiologbon (see p. 120)
14. Ika (see p. 122)
15. Obeogunda (see p. 124)
16. Alafia (see p. 125)

As you go through the worksheet, come back to this page to find your corresponding Odu names. Write that Odu name in the space provided in the worksheet, and then go to the corresponding page number in the Interpretation of Birth Odus section in order to learn more!

Major Houses

◗ *House One: Odu Ori*

Add together all digits in birth date, reducing sum to 16 or fewer. Write the Odu that corresponds with your answer in the space below.

____ + ____ + _____ +_____ +_____ +_____ +_____ +_____ = _____
day   day   month month   year   year   year   year

If it is greater than 16, make the reduction: _____ + _____ = _____

My birth Odu Ori is (see page 161) _____.

Relates to: Identity and Personality

Interpreting Your Birth Odus (beginning on page 100) has detailed descriptions of each Odu. You can use the space below to take notes about your Odu's description and what it means to you.

❶ *House Two: Oju Ori*

Create two columns of birth date as shown below. Add up each column separately, reducing to 16 or fewer if necessary. Write the Odu that corresponds with the sum in the space below.

```
_____D_____   |   _____ D_____
_____M_____   |   _____ M_____
_____Y_____   |   _____ Y_____
_____Y_____   |   _____ Y_____
```

The sum already reduced in the left column is _____, so the Odu that corresponds to my Oju Ori (see page 161) _____.

Relates to: Temperament and Intellect

Interpreting Your Birth Odus (beginning on page 100) has detailed descriptions of each Odu. You can use the space below to take notes about your Odu's description and what it means to you.

🌑 *House Three: Ikoko Ori*

From the previous step, write the Odu that corresponds with your answer from the right column in the space below.

The sum already reduced in the column on the right is _____, and hence the Odu that corresponds to my Ikoko Ori is (see page 161) _____.

Relates to: Personal Evolution

Interpreting Your Birth Odus (beginning on page 100) has detailed descriptions of each Odu. You can use the space below to take notes about your Odu's description and what it means to you.

◖ *House Four: Apá Òtún*

Add together your Odu Ori and your Ikoko Ori, reduce that number if it is more than 16. Write the Odu that corresponds with your answer in the space below.

_____ + _____ = _____

If it is greater than 16, make the reduction: _____ + _____ = _____

With that, my Odu in Apá Òtún is (see page 161) _____.

Relates to: Material World, Career, and Finance

Interpreting Your Birth Odus (beginning on page 100) has detailed descriptions of each Odu. You can use the space below to take notes about your Odu's description and what it means to you.

◐ *House Five: Apá Osi*

Add together your totals for Odu Ori + Ikoko Ori + Apá Òtún, reduce to 16 or fewer if necessary. Write the corresponding Odu in the space below.

_____ + _____ + _____ = _____

Reduce to 16 or fewer

_____ + _____ = _____

With that, my Odu in Apá Osi is (see page 161) _____.

Relates to: Relationships, Affection, and Sexual Life

Interpreting Your Birth Odus (beginning on page 100) has detailed descriptions of each Odu. You can use the space below to take notes about your Odu's description and what it means to you.

🝔 *House Six: Osogbo Ori (Negative Odu)*

Add together all the previous totals, reducing to 16 or fewer if necessary. Write the corresponding Odu in the space below.

_____ + _____ + _____ + _____ = _____

Making the reduction, if necessary: _____ + _____ = _____

With that, my Odu in Osogbo Ori is (see page 161) _____.

Relates to: Challenges and Inner Revolution

Interpreting Your Birth Odus (beginning on page 100) has detailed descriptions of each Odu. You can use the space below to take notes about your Odu's description and what it means to you.

Minor Houses

There are two options for calculating the Odus of the minor houses: obtaining a single Odu for each quadrant, which is the simplified way to do it, or obtaining two Odus per quadrant, identifying both a positive and a negative aspect of the house in question, thereby engaging in a deeper analysis. With the following instructions you can try either or both methods.

Quadrant One

- Do I plan the steps needed to get where I want to go?
- Are my efforts valued by others and myself?
- Do I work at a profession I like, and does my work give me pleasure?
- Do I apply my main positive characteristics in building a responsible and committed image?

Add Oju Ori + Apá Òtún; if the sum is larger than 16, add those digits and find the corresponding Odu.

_____ (Oju Ori) + _____ (Apá Òtún) = _____

Reducing if necessary: _____ + _____ = _____

My quadrant one Odu is _____ (see page 161).

For a deeper analysis, you can calculate separate Odus for positive and negative aspects of quadrant one. After you determine your Odus through calculation, you will find them in the Interpretations of Birth Odus section beginning on page 100 and only look at the positive or negative expressions.

Positive: Odu Ori + Oju Ori + Apá Òtún

_____ + _____ + _____ = _____

My quadrant one positive Odu is (see page 161) _____ .

Negative: Osogbo Ori + Oju Ori + Apá Òtún

_____ + _____ + _____ = _____

My quadrant one negative Odu is (see page 161) _____ .

◖ Quadrant Two

- Do I do what must be done to get where I want to be?
- Do I seek to improve myself professionally and intellectually, taking courses and improving my skills, to grow in my career?
- Am I able to fulfill a schedule of tasks without outside activities taking my focus?
- How do I act today to achieve the goals I set for myself tomorrow?

Add Apá Òtún + Ikoko Ori; if the sum is larger than 16, further reduce to find the corresponding Odu.

_____ (Apá Òtún) + _____ (Ikoko Ori) = _____

Reducing if necessary: _____ + _____ = _____

My quadrant two Odu is _____ (see page 161).

For a deeper analysis, you can calculate separate Odus for positive and negative aspects of quadrant two. After you determine your Odus through calculation, you will find them in the Interpretations of Birth Odus section beginning on page 100 and only look at the positive or negative expressions.

Positive: Odu Ori + Apá Òtún + Ikoko Ori

Insert _____ + _____ + _____ = _____

My quadrant two positive Odu is (see page 161) _____.

Negative: Osogbo Ori + Apá Òtún + Ikoko Ori

Insert _____ + _____ + _____ = _____

My quadrant two negative Odu is (see page 161) _____.

◑ *Quadrant Three*

- Do I expose my opinions, desires, and wishes to others while respecting theirs?
- Do I recognize my own worth and my limitations, not allowing others' opinions to interfere with how I perceive myself?
- Do I understand what my true role is in the lives of the people I live with and what their roles are in mine and avoid crossing boundaries or inverting social roles and functions?
- Do I express my positive and negative feelings in a balanced way, honestly but not aggressively?
- Can I receive both criticism and praise?

Add Oju Ori + Apá Osi; if the sum is larger than 16, further reduce to find the corresponding Odu.

_____ (Oju Ori) + _____ (Apá Osi) = _____

Reducing if necessary: _____ + _____ = _____

My quadrant three Odu is _____ (see page 161).

For a deeper analysis, you can calculate separate Odus for positive and negative aspects of quadrant three. After you determine your Odus through calculation, you will find them in the Interpretations of Birth Odus section beginning on page 100 and only look at the positive or negative expressions.

Positive: Odu Ori + Oju Ori + Apá Osi

Insert _____ + _____ + _____ = _____

My quadrant three positive Odu is (see page 161) _____.

Negative: Osogbo Ori + Oju Ori + Apá Osi

Insert _____ + _____ + _____ = _____

My quadrant three negative Odu is (see page 161) _____.

◗ *Quadrant Four*

- Do I accept my physical body as it is without guilt?
- Do I actively take care of my physical and mental health, seeking to develop healthy habits?
- Do I respect the sexual and affective desires, fantasies, and limits of the people around me, at the same time as I try to fulfill my desires and fantasies in a balanced way?
- Do I pay attention to each person who passes my way, treating him or her with respect and recognition, regardless of his or her social or financial status?
- Do my attitudes, my tone of voice, and my way of behaving convey aggression or acceptance?
- Do I know how to recognize and act when a relationship—social, professional, familial, or love—proves to be toxic or harmful, or do I remain stuck in it even when it hurts me?

Add Apá Osi + Ikoko Ori; if the sum is larger than 16, further reduce to find the corresponding Odu.

_____ (Apá Osi) + _____ (Ikoko Ori) = _____

Reducing if necessary: _____ + _____ = _____

My quadrant four Odu is _____ (see page 161).

For a deeper analysis, you can calculate separate Odus for positive and negative aspects of quadrant four. After you determine your Odus through calculation, you will find them in the Interpretations of Birth Odus section beginning on page 100 and only look at the positive or negative expressions.

Positive: Odu Ori + Apá Osi + Ikoko Ori

Insert ____ + ____ + ____ = ____

My quadrant four positive Odu is (see page 161) _____.

Negative: Osogbo Ori + Apá Osi + Ikoko Ori

Insert ____ + ____ + ____ = ____

My quadrant four negative Odu is (see page 161) _____.

References

Barros, José Flávio Pessoa de, and Maria Lina Leão Teixeira. 1989. "O Código do Corpo: Inscrições e Marcas dos Orixás," in Carlos Eugenio Marcondes de Moura, *Meu Sinal Está no Teu Corpo: Escritos Sobre a Religião Dos Orixás*. São Paulo, Brazil: Edicon-Edusp.

Beniste, José. 2012. *Jogo de Búzios: Um Encontro com o Desconhecido*. Rio de Janeiro, Brazil: Bertrand Brasil.

Eyin, Cido de Oxum. 2014. *Okutá: A Pedra Sagrada que Encanta Orixá*. São Paulo, Brazil: Alfabeto.

Filho, Nelson Pires, and Wagner Veneziani Costa. 2016. *Jogo de Búzios e o Culto a Ifá*. São Paulo, Brazil: Madras.

Martins, Adilson Antônio. 2013. *O Jogo de Búzios por Odu*. Rio de Janeiro, Brazil: Pallas.

Napoleão, Eduardo. 2011. *Vocabulário Yorùbá*. Rio de Janeiro, Brazil: Pallas.

Oxóssi, Diego de. 2018. *Desvendando Exu: O Guardião dos Caminhos*. São Paulo, Brazil: Arole Cultural.

———. 2019. *O Poder das Folhas: Banhos, Defumações e Magias*. São Paulo, Brazil: Arole Cultural.

———. 2020. *O Segredo das Folhas: Magia Prática para o Dia-a-Dia*. São Paulo, Brazil: Arole Cultural.

Prandi, Reginaldo. 2001. *Mitologia dos Orixás*. São Paulo, Brazil: Companhia das Letras.

Ribeiro, Carlos, and Vilson Caetano de Souza Jr. 2018. *Comida de Santo que Se Come*. São Paulo, Brazil: Arole Cultural.

Santos, Maria Stella de Azevedo. 2013. *Ofun*. Salvador, Brazil: Assembleia Legislativa do Estado da Bahia.

Silva, Vagner Gonçalves da. 2015. *Exu: O Guardião da Casa do Futuro*. Rio de Janeiro, Brazil: Pallas.

Varanda, Jorge Alberto. 2011. *O Destino Revelado no Jogo de Búzios.* 2nd ed. Editora Eco.

Verger, P. F. 1995. Ewé: the use of plants in Yoruba society. São Paulo: Companhia das Letras.

———. 2012. Nota sobre o culto aos Orixás e Voduns na Bahia de Todos os Santos, no Brasil, e na Antiga Costa dos Escravos, na África. Trad. Carlos Eugênio Marcondes de Moura. São Paulo: EDUSP.

———. 2002. Orixás: deuses iorubas na África e no novo mundo. Trad. Cida Nóbrega. Salvador: Corrupio.

Vieira, Paulo. 2017. *O Poder da Autorresponsabilidade.* São Paulo, Brazil: Editora Gente.

Index

Page numbers in *italics* refer to illustrations.

About the Author

Diego de Oxóssi, based in São Paulo, Brazil, graduated with a degree in management processes from Anhembi Morumbi University and Integral Systemic Coaching at Febracis coaching institution. He is a priest of Kimbanda and a babalosha of Candomblé and has provided personal development, consulting, and spiritual guidance throughout Brazil and abroad. For more than twenty years, he has been dedicated to researching and presenting courses, lectures, and workshops on Afro-Brazilian religions, their regional forms of expression, and the integration of their rituals into society.

In 2015, he published his first book, *Desvendando Exu,* which was published in English as *Traditional Brazilian Black Magic* (Rochester, Vt.: Destiny Books, 2021), in which he demystifies Eshu, a controversial character of African-based religions, and shows that, despite Eshu's erroneous syncretism with the devil, he is the biggest friend, defender, and companion of his faithful. Between 2016 and 2018, Diego wrote and published in Portuguese the trilogy *As Folhas Sagradas,* a bestselling series in Brazil, which was published in English as *Sacred Leaves: A Magical Guide to Orisha Herbal Witchcraft* (Woodbury, Minn.: Llewellyn, 2022).

In 2019, Diego de Oxóssi was awarded the Young Talent of the Editorial Market award by PublishNews, the largest communication vehicle in the sector, and has participated in international book fairs in London, Bologna, Buenos Aires, and Frankfurt. He is editor in chief of Editora Arole Cultural, a Brazilian publishing house specializing in African Brazilian and African American spirituality books.

Learn more about the author at www.diegodeoxossi.com.br